# Financing Your Equestrian Activities: Sponsorships and Scholarships

Suzanne K. B. Fraser

*Equissentials Press*

Library of Congress Catalog Card Number: 96-90853

Fraser, Suzanne K. B.
      Financing Your Equestrian Activities – Sponsorships and Scholarships

ISBN 0-9654900-0-9

Cover photo by Ed Camelli, courtesy of *Practical Horseman* magazine.

# ଓଃ **Dedication** ଃଡ଼

To my parents

*Linton P. Bell and Sally C. Bell*

and my husband

*Douglas A. Fraser*

# Acknowledgements

Special thanks go to:

- my husband *Doug* for the incredible amount of time he spent solving hardware and software problems, running errands, and acting as personal secretary

- my very special friend *Susan S. Sellew* for her generous help in my riding and writing endeavors

- *Natasha Grigg* for her editorial contributions

- my stepdaughter *Sara B. Fraser* for her editorial contributions

- my longtime friend, fellow horsewoman, and inspiration, *Patricia L. Goodman* for doing such an excellent job of interviewing and photographing Richard Rader

- *Joan Del Genio* who came in toward the end of the project and cleaned up all the loose ends

- *Ellen Epstein* for her publishing and marketing expertise

- *Michael Maddalena* and *Rebecca Siegel* for their assistance in page design, and *Rebecca* for her editorial contributions

Sincere thanks to the individuals and organizations listed below who so generously provided me with information and encouragement.

Charee Adams, American Trakehner Association
American Driving Society
American Quarter Horse Foundation
American Quarter Horse Youth Association
Mrs. C-H Asmis, Carl-Heinrich Asmis Scholarship Fund
K. Dwayne Beck, Palomino Horse Breeders of America
Dane Bettes, American Morgan Horse Institute
Haley Blacklow, Stateline Tack
Amy L. Burns, American Saddlebred Horse Association Foundation
    Scholarship
Jim Cada, International Arabian Horse Foundation

Marindi & Mick Coward
John Craven, Miller Harness Company
Diana DeRosa
Diana Deterding
Sally Dunn
Jennifer Emrich, American Horse Shows Association
Kathleen Fallon, American Horse Shows Association
Violet Forbes, United States Equestrian Team
Sharon Gallagher, United States Combined Training Association
Matt & Stacy Gallien
Marie and Michelle Gibson
Robin J. Gifford, United States Dressage Foundation, Inc.
Jay Goldberg, The SportsMakers Agency, L.L.C.
Sue Greenall
John Hamilton, The Dymar Agency
Ruth Hogan-Poulsen
Cecelia Hoyt
Ing. Loro Piana & C.
Gina Johnson, Stadium Jumping, Inc.
Valerie Kanavy
Jean Kelley, Pony of the Americas Club Scholarship Endowment Fund, Inc.
Lisa Kulski
Richard E. Kurzeja, International Buckskin Horse Foundation
Lisa L. Landis, Welsh Pony & Cob Society of America
Lisa M. LeBlanc
Mark Leone
Donald V. Little, Jr.
William Long
Jack Lowry, Dodge Truck Rodeo
Sean E. Lyles, Professional Rodeo Cowboys Association
John Lyons
Linda Matthews, National Reining Horse Association
Carole Meyer-Webster
Keri Minden, Appaloosa Youth Foundation Scholarship Committee
Andrea Moore, American Horse Shows Association
Mickey Morrison, American Endurance Ride Conference
Beezie Patton
Lisa Peterson, American Morgan Horse Association
Trez Cattie Pomilo, *Practical Horseman*
Larry Poulin
Karen Powell, The Pinewood Corporation
Professional Rodeo Cowboys Association

Holly Pulsifer
Richard Rader
Karen Reid, Foxfire Farm
Jackie Richardson
Ed Roberts, American Paint Horse Association
Susan Russell
Kathy Schultz, American Hackney Horse Society
Richard and Lee Ann Shrake
Terry Schroeder, Dodge Truck Rodeo
Debbie Shaffner Stephens
Gary Tunnison, The Dressage Foundation, Inc.
Linda Van Ceylon
Ruth Van Horn
Mark H. Walter, Beval Ltd.
Russell Webster
Welsh Pony and Cob Foundation
Sue and Terry Williams, Williamsburg Farm
Barbara Wolff

# Preface

This book is for the many devoted horse people whose goals exceed their budgets. It takes more than just talent to succeed in the horse world. Sufficient financial backing is essential to the continuing success of any horseperson.

My interest is in competing at the FEI levels in dressage, but lack of finances prompted me to explore sponsorship. I was aware of sponsorships for jumper riders, but had only heard of a few dressage riders being sponsored. It made me wonder about western, polo, eventing, driving, and the other disciplines. Was there much, if anything, available in the way of sponsorship money in these areas? And how did sponsorships differ from one discipline to another? How did people find sponsors? Keep sponsors? Present themselves to potential sponsors? Myriad other questions followed.

These questions inspired me to seek the answers and see if I could organize information that would be of value to other horse people. Hence this book.

I started out by developing two questionnaires: one for sponsors and the other for sponsored riders. Then I drafted a list of every sponsored rider I had ever read about or heard about. This was followed by hours of phone interviews, which often led to names of other people to contact. Through these interviews, my questions were answered. Among the many important things I learned were: there are many different types of sponsorships and methods for finding sponsors, and sponsored riders and sponsors are more than willing to share their experiences with people who show a sincere interest.

While exploring how people raise money to pursue their riding exploits, I became cognizant of the many scholarship funds available throughout the country. Thus, an entire section of this book is devoted to the different types of scholarships — riding, educational, and award — with information gathered from the organizations that offer scholarships. Scholarship funds are growing in number, and there are undoubtedly new funds that have sprouted since the publication of this book.

Some of the horse people in the following pages will be immediately recognizable to you while others are not yet widely known. But each has an interesting and unique story that may bring you closer to formulating a plan of your own for obtaining sponsorship.

Best wishes to you in your equine endeavors and in your efforts to find sponsorship.

# Contents

## The Elements of Sponsorship     13

Getting Started     15

The Five Ps     19

Getting What You Want: Asking is the Key     23

Creating a Proposal     27

Pitfalls to Avoid, Dealing with Rejection, and the Time Element     33

## The Sponsored Riders     37

Newspaper Article Secures Grand Prix Horse
for Michelle Gibson     39

Debbie Shaffner Stephens Asks "What Can I Do
For My Sponsor?"     45

Marindi Coward Thinks and Acts Creatively to Find
Sponsorship     49

Donald V. Little Jr. Espouses the Value of Networking     55

Mark Leone is Sponsored by Italian and Canadian Companies     59

Valerie Kanavy Demonstrates Team Spirit     67

Ruth Hogan-Poulsen Seeks Sponsorship Abroad     73

Beezie Patton Projects the Right Image     79

Richard Rader's Friends Help Spread the Word     85

Lisa Kulski Finds Sponsors Without Actively Looking     91

Richard Shrake's Dual Roles as Sponsored Rider and Sponsor     97

## The Sponsors     105

Know Thy Sponsor     107

The Right Demographics Influence Corporate Sponsors     111

Miller Harness Company Backs Riders with Staying Power 115

Beval, Ltd. Sponsors Events and Individuals 117

Natasha Grigg Enjoys Sponsoring a Friend 121

A Message From the Sponsors 127

The Value of Event Sponsorship 129

Rodeo Events Appeal to Corporate Sponsors 133

## Sports Agents, Insurance, Rules & Restrictions 137

Using an Agency to Secure Sponsorship 139

Insurance 143

Rules and Restrictions for Sponsored Riders 145

## Scholarships 149

Scholarships 151

Riding Club Scholarship Funds 153

Educational Riding Scholarships 157

Educational Scholarships Through Breed Organizations 161

Scholarships as Awards 171

Final Note 175

# The Elements of Sponsorship

# Getting Started

Almost every horse person is confronted with the challenge of managing the enormous expense involved in maintaining, training, and competing horses. The purchase price of a quality horse is only the first and not always the most significant expense. Upkeep, training, and competition costs are high no matter what discipline you pursue.

Many riders cannot make enough money either within or outside of the horse industry to cover the costs, so more and more are finding help in the form of sponsorships: from friends, family, students, anonymous sponsors, or corporate sponsors.

Whether the sponsor is private or corporate, the variation in sponsorship arrangements is as vast as it is creative. Some arrangements are short term, for a limited amount of money, and some are for indefinite time periods with all expenses paid. Several American riders have even succeeded in finding sponsorship with European companies.

Sponsors can be directly related to the horse industry (the owner of a breeding stallion who wants his horse capably represented in competition) or they may have nothing at all to do with horses (a merchant who sells a non-horse related product).

Sponsorships are attained in two ways: by riders actively seeking sponsorship or by sponsors offering their assistance to riders who they feel are deserving or can do something for them in exchange. There are numerous instances of students sponsoring their instructors, friends sponsoring friends, and so on.

For the majority of riders who have to actively seek sponsorship, it is necessary to have a plan with clearly defined goals, time frames, and a statement of the benefits to a prospective sponsor.

## ■ ■ ■ Understanding What Motivates Sponsors

To understand the premise behind sponsorship, it is important to understand what motivates sponsors.

**Private sponsors** – Private sponsors provide sponsorship for some or all of the following reasons:

- love of the sport

- love of horses

- prestige

- interest in a particular rider

- the enjoyment of owning a winning horse

- the fun of traveling around the country or the world to watch their horse compete

- profit potential

Private sponsors are generally not as concerned with name recognition as are corporate sponsors. Instead, they derive enjoyment from watching their horse and rider develop and compete.

**Corporate sponsors** – Companies sponsor equestrians for one or more of the following reasons:

- to increase their sales

- to increase their visibility

- to educate consumers about their products and how they differ from the competition's

- to showcase their products in an upscale market

Corporate sponsors look for riders who are consistent performers, articulate, and able to promote their products.

## ■ ■ ■ Generating Interest

Whether you are seeking a corporate or a private sponsor, you must generate interest by educating sponsors on how they will benefit by sponsoring you. You will need to create a proposal and a budget as described in the section entitled *Creating a Proposal.*

# The Five Ps

When reading about a sponsored rider, it's easy to think how lucky that person is. But luck rarely has much to do with finding sponsorship. Aside from their obvious skill, sponsored riders all seem to subscribe to the same five principles, which I refer to as the five Ps: Positioning, Participation, Presentation, Positive Attitude, and Perseverance.

## ■ ■ ■ Positioning

Positioning oneself for opportunity is essential to the success of any endeavor. Positioning means developing a strategy that repeatedly places you in the public eye.

It doesn't matter how skilled you are if no one knows who you are. Successful sponsorees unanimously recommend that you seize every opportunity to meet and talk with anyone who might be able to help you or refer you to someone who can. Dressage rider Ruth Hogan-Poulsen describes her efforts to find sponsorship as "an ongoing process of going to shows, clinics, and other horse-related activities and speaking with anyone and everyone who would listen."

Don't be shy about making your goals known to as many people as possible. Get yourself written up in the newspaper, an equine journal, a business magazine or anywhere else that a potential sponsor might read about you. (See the chapter entitled *Newspaper Article Secures Grand Prix Horse for Michelle Gibson* for a case study).

## ■ ■ ■ Participation

Participating in competitions, demonstrations, clinics, and other horse-related activities allows you to meet people, demonstrate your skill, and make your goals known to individuals or corporate representatives who might be able to help you. Volunteering at shows or on committees is also a good method for meeting people and developing name recognition for yourself.

Ownership of a horse is not requisite to participation. There are always horses available to competent and conscientious riders for numerous reasons: owners who are on vacation, traveling on business, too involved with family to give their horses the attention they need, and so on. These people will often gratefully turn over the reins to a talented rider.

It can be very beneficial to align yourself with a reputable boarding facility where you can meet boarders who may need help keeping their horses in work. Each time you demonstrate that you can and will do well by an owner, your opportunities for other rides increase. One rider told me, "I had a friend who could not ride her horse on a daily basis and invited me to ride him at the boarding facility at which she kept him. Other riders started asking me to work their horses, and before long, there were more horses to ride than I could actually accommodate. Also, I have been able to show some of these horses at their owner's expense."

## ■ ■ ■ Presentation

Making a good presentation is paramount. Presentation is not only the way you and your horse are turned out, but also the performance you deliver. This is the memory that people will take home with them and what may cause one of them to sponsor you at a future date.

Good turnout is everything from an impeccably groomed and braided horse, to shiny boots and immaculate clothes. Skill alone cannot make up for the distraction caused by dirty boots, a poor braiding job, or the like. What meets the eye has to be pleasing even if it means staying up until after midnight to get everything just right for the next day.

Presentation is not something to be concerned with only on the day of the show. Your day-to-day presentation and care of your horse tells people a lot about your commitment and conscientiousness. Many riders have found sponsors from boarders or students at the barns where they ride; sponsors who see them on a regular basis and are *repeatedly* impressed by what they see.

## ■■■ Positive Attitude

A positive attitude is important for obtaining the support of a sponsor. By watching top riders train and compete, you will quickly discover that it is much more than just their riding ability that makes them successful. They have positive attitudes that enable them to cope gracefully with difficult situations. These are the real success stories. These are the riders who perform at a consistently high level and are able to secure sponsorship. You will meet and learn about these unique individuals later on in this book.

## ■■■ Perseverance

Perseverance is probably the most difficult of the five Ps. It is the ability to pursue your goal no matter how difficult or discouraging the circumstances. It is human nature to abhor rejection and try to avoid it. But if you are serious about looking for a sponsor, then you will have to learn how to cope with rejection. Anyone who helps raise money for charities will tell you how discouraging it can be. There are usually far more no's than yes's, and you have to have the fortitude to keep going in spite of negative responses. With the exception of the few people who had sponsorship offered to them, not a single sponsoree interviewed said that finding sponsorship was easy. Those who actively sought sponsorship received numerous no's. But what every one of them said after finding sponsorship was that it was well worth the effort.

# Getting What You Want:
# Asking is the Key

Six important things you need to know about asking are:

1. ask the right people    4. get out of your comfort zone
2. ask at the right time    5. be persistent
3. ask in the right way    6. be specific

## ■ ■ ■ Ask the Right People

Ask everyone you know – friends, relatives, business associates – and everyone you can find out about: friends of friends, friends of relatives, friends of business associates, and companies that could benefit from a sponsorship situation. Although many of these people will not be in a position to help you, a number of them will be able to direct you to people who can. The more people who know about your plan, the more likely you are to find someone who can and will help.

### ■ ■ ■ Ask at the Right Time

You need to choose the right time to ask to avoid disrupting the lives of the people you are contacting. When calling prospective sponsors, be sure to ask if you are catching them at a good time after introducing yourself. If not, ask them when would be a convenient time for them to speak with you. This call will be one of the first impressions you make on a potential sponsor, so be sure that the impression you make is a good one.

### ■ ■ ■ Ask the Right Way

The right way to ask is politely and with sincerity. It's that simple. Projecting sincerity is easy when you believe in what you are doing. Even though you may have occasional doubts about your ability to find a sponsor, it is important to project confidence when speaking with people who are in a position to help.

It can be uncomfortable to ask for help because some people are going to say no and nobody likes rejection. Your first task is to acknowledge the fact that some people will refuse to help, but their refusal will usually have nothing to do with you personally. Some people won't be in a position to help, while others just won't find an equestrian sponsorship appealing.

If a sponsorship is the only way you can afford your equestrian pursuits and you are committed to this endeavor, you have to find the courage to ask.

Ask nicely and be willing to accept "no" graciously. Always thank the person for having taken the time to review your proposal or talk with you in person. Their time is valuable and they have done you a service by listening to you. You may also find that they can offer valuable advice or refer you to someone else who might be able to help. Every contact you make leads you closer to your goal.

### ■ ■ ■ Get Out of Your Comfort Zone

Much is said and written about the psychology of competitive sports and the necessary mental and physical preparation. Asking for help requires mental preparation and a willingness to get out of your comfort zone.

If you remember what it was like when you were first learning to ride, you will remember how "uncomfortable" it was in the beginning. I don't necessarily mean physically uncomfortable, but uncomfortable in general. Trying to make your body do what your instructor was telling you, acclimating yourself to the horse, trying to gain some control in what seemed like an out-of-control situation, and coping with the fears associated with competing. But you persevered through this incredible discomfort because of that special feeling you have for horses. Not only did you succeed in mastering the basics of horsemanship, but more importantly, you succeeded in getting out of your comfort zone.

In time, you became comfortable keeping your leg in the proper position, sitting deep, keeping your hands low, steering, stopping, and sending the horse forward. You learned the aids for different transitions, and once you had that down, your instructor once again delighted in making you uncomfortable by insisting that you make smoother transitions, ride the horse more forward, and perform more advanced movements. Then, your instructor taught you to ride more challenging horses because instructors know all about comfort zones; maybe not in those terms, but they know. Then you did advanced movements on the more challenging horses. Again, you could do it because you had learned through experience that you could succeed even when you were uncomfortable.

Any new challenge or endeavor is going to take you out of your comfort zone. Until you are willing to repeatedly be uncomfortable, you won't be able to progress. However, in time, your asking skills will improve just the way your equestrian skills improved enabling you to achieve your goals.

## ■ ■ ■ Persist

Follow up on any and all leads, and don't get discouraged or quit because of negative responses. Be willing to contact people more than once unless they have clearly and unequivocally stated that they are not going to help you.

## ■ ■ ■ Be Specific About What You Ask For

The reason that an entire section of this book is devoted to creating a proposal is to encourage you to state concisely what you need, when you need it, and how much it will cost. If you do not have this information available, it is almost impossible for anyone to help you. For instance, if you approach someone and say, "I need some money for my riding," you may be given some money. But since you did not state how much you need, you may be offered $100 and at some future date. It was a nice gesture from the person offering it, but obviously won't get you much closer to your goal unless your specific plan is to ask 500 people for exactly $100 each. And this is still not specific enough. Be sure to tell them *when* you need the money.

### ■ ■ ■ Create and Maintain a Vision of Your Goal

Have a vision of your desired goal and continually remind yourself of that goal. It will give you the momentum you need to follow through, and your passion for your pursuits will be evident to the people you are asking. It's your enthusiasm and commitment along with your equestrian skill that will make people want to sponsor you.

Visualize in your own mind exactly what you want to have happen, how you want it to happen, and what you will do when it does happen. Imagine a person saying, "Yes, my company will sponsor you." Then visualize yourself successfully negotiating a difficult water hazard in a driving competition, or negotiating a course of jumps at the Washington International with your sponsored horse. These positive images will help you stay focused on your goal.

### ■ ■ ■ The "I've Asked But Not Received" Problem

If what you are doing is consistently not working, spending more time and energy in the same vein will net you the same result. Take the time to learn why you have not received the help you are seeking.

If you have done a lot of asking and gotten some results, even though they may be small, then you *are* doing something right. Focus on what that something is and do more of it. Equally important is to determine what techniques are not working and abandon them. To find out what people do and don't like about your proposal, *ask.*

Be creative, and try new approaches. Re-use what works, abandon what doesn't, and be willing to experiment.

# Creating a Proposal

Proposals to a prospective sponsor can be as simple as a letter or a conversation or as elaborate as an entire package including a cover letter, plan, resume, budget, competition record, testimonials, and photo or video. The main purpose of the proposal is to convince a prospective sponsor that your endeavor is worthwhile and that they will benefit in some way by helping you.

## ■■■ Who Needs to do a Proposal and Why?

Everyone. Although sponsorees' opinions vary widely as to the value of proposals for actually securing sponsorship, there is no question that you will benefit by creating one for some or all of the following reasons:

- It gives you the opportunity to clarify your goals to yourself and to your sponsor.
- Through the proposal you will specify what actions you are going to take to achieve your goals.
- It will shed light on some areas that you may have overlooked.

- You will create a budget, which is essential to both you and your sponsor.

- It will help you identify what you can provide a sponsor.

- It is something you can mail ahead of time to a potential sponsor to introduce yourself.

- If you approach people face-to-face, the proposal is something you can leave with them to peruse at their leisure.

- A proposal shows that you have given a lot of thought to your plan and are prepared to move forward once you have the funds.

- You will be better able to answer a potential sponsor's questions by having gone through the exercise of creating a proposal.

- It clarifies the time frame of your plan.

## ■ ■ ■ What Should be Included in the Proposal?

### Cover Letter

Studies by direct mail marketers indicate that most people read the first and last paragraphs of cover letters. If something catches their interest, they will read the body of the letter. If you are seeking corporate sponsorship, it is important to understand that you are contacting busy executives who don't have time to waste, therefore, it is vital that you make your point quickly.

The cover letter should be short (preferably one page) and concise. You want to pique the reader's curiosity and inspire his/her confidence. Therefore, you must write with self-confidence. Tell your reader in the first paragraph why you are contacting him/her and how he/she will benefit by helping you. The body of the letter should briefly explain your plan. Invite questions and indicate your willingness to meet with prospective sponsors at their convenience.

Close the letter by telling your reader what follow-up action you will take; a date and time that you will call to see if they are interested in your plan. Be sure to follow through and call on the date you indicated in your letter.

Several sponsorees had success sending handwritten letters to potential *private* sponsors. They were in agreement that the personal touch helped. However, in the case of corporate sponsors, it is advisable to type the cover letter. Be sure that your name, address, and phone number are on the letter.

## Plan

The plan should include, but not be limited to, the following components:

- an introduction telling the sponsor what you are asking for
- a description of the discipline you are involved in
- a clear statement of your goals
- a description of how you will achieve your goals
- a description of the type of horse(s) needed for this discipline, or a description of the horse(s) you have
- your training plans
- your competition plans – whenever possible, include fact sheets on specific shows where you will be competing
- where you will be based
- the time frame of the plan
- why a sponsor should pick you (e.g., your competition record, the horses you have available to you, etc.)
- details of how the sponsor will benefit by sponsoring you

    When approaching corporate sponsors, explain how their company will benefit by sponsoring you

    When approaching private sponsors, explain how satisfying it will be for them to watch their horse as he progresses in his training and wins in competition, and how much fun it will be traveling to different places to see him perform

Be clear about what you are offering and be sure that you can follow through with everything you say you will do for your sponsor. If eight shows are the most you can do in a season, don't mislead a prospective sponsor into believing that you can do more.

## Your Resume

Important components of the resume are:

- your name, address, phone number, fax number, and e-mail address if applicable
- your educational background with horses

- information on your training background as well as who you currently train with
- any special certifications or awards that you have earned
- competition record

Additional information may include hobbies, education, employment history. Include any or all of these if they apply in any way to your sponsor's line of products.

If you have something unique to offer a sponsor, draw their attention to that uniqueness. (For example, if hiking is one of your hobbies, and you are seeking sponsorship from a company that manufactures or sells hiking boots, be sure to bring your hobby to their attention).

## Budget

The budget is one of the most important components in your proposal. Be sure to prepare a budget that covers all of the anticipated costs and is broken down according to the time frame of the sponsorship. See the following example for some ideas on preparing a budget. No detail is too small when preparing a budget. Be completely honest with yourself about actual costs so that there won't be any unpleasant surprises at some future date.

### A Sample Budget

| Item | Year One | Year Two | Total |
|------|----------|----------|-------|
| Purchase Price | $50,000 | N/A | $50,000 |
| Board | 6,000 | 6,500 | 12,500 |
| Blacksmith | 1,200 | 1,500 | 2,700 |
| Veterinary | 1,000 | 1,000 | 2,000 |
| Training | 2,800 | 3,500 | 6,300 |
| Equipment | 2,000 | 1,000 | 3,000 |
| Competitions | 6,300 | 7,000 | 13,300 |
| TOTAL | $69,300 | $20,500 | $ 89,800 |

The above sample budget accounts for inflation on Year Two. This is a very simple budget for a short time period, but it does include major expense items except for insurance.

You should create detailed work sheets that break down the expenses on a per month basis. Work sheets will help you establish figures that truly reflect your needs, and they will be useful in the future to see how close you are staying to your proposed budget.

## Your Competition Record

If your competition record is extensive, include it as a separate document. List awards chronologically, with the most recent listed first.

### Testimonials

Personal references as well as testimonials from trainers, students, judges, and other equine professionals are valuable additions to your proposal.

### Videos and Photographs of Yourself

A good quality color photograph enhances the appearance of your proposal and is more tangible than pages of text describing your ability and past record.

A video, if well done, is a useful marketing tool. It does not need to be more than 10 minutes, but exceptional quality is a must. A poor quality video will do you more harm than no video at all.

Videotaping horses is much trickier than most other types of videography. Be sure you hire someone with experience videotaping horses. A good place to find a suitable videographer is at one of the larger shows in your area. It is common for videographers to attend and record competitions for riders.

## ■■■ Be Specific About What You Can Offer A Corporate Sponsor

In order to get a corporate sponsor interested, you must tell them how they will benefit by sponsoring you. The following services and information are among those that you could offer your sponsor:

- display your sponsor's name on your trailer, tack box, saddle pad, etc.

- wear clothing that shows your sponsor's logo

- prefix your horse's name with the sponsor's name

- provide your sponsor with fact sheets from competitions you will be entering (fact sheets are obtained from the organizers of the larger shows and include information such as the date and location of the competition, the number of spectators anticipated, the number of horses competing, media coverage, prize money, trade booth opportunities, etc.)

- provide your sponsor with demographic information on the horse industry (see the chapter entitled *The Right Demographics Influence Sponsors*)

- display their product, if appropriate

- if your sponsor has a booth at a show you are competing at, be willing to visit the booth to sign autographs and answer questions

- attend your sponsor's promotional events and speak with people interested in your sponsor's product

- apprise your sponsor of any potential news media opportunities

### Follow-Up

It is your responsibility to call people after submitting your proposal. The purpose of the call is to make sure that they have received your proposal and to see if you can set up a face-to-face meeting where you can describe your plan in more detail and answer any questions they may have.

It is advisable to call within two to three weeks of sending the proposal. In this way, the proposal has had sufficient time to reach its recipient, but has not been sitting in a pile long enough to be completely forgotten.

## ■ ■ ■ A Note on Follow-up Calls and Corporate Sponsors

Many of the follow-up calls you make will elicit a negative response. Be sure to thank the person for reviewing your materials, but don't hang up yet. Ask that person if he/she knows of anyone who may be interested in your proposal. It is important that you not overlook any sponsorship opportunities and networking is a powerful way of making contacts. See the chapter entitled *Donald V. Little Jr. Espouses the Value of Networking* for an excellent example of the value of networking.

Numerous riders, including Olympic dressage rider Michelle Gibson, tried without success to find corporate sponsorship through direct mailings. The few people who had some success had one significant factor in their favor – they knew someone within the company they were approaching.

# Pitfalls to Avoid, Dealing with Rejection, and the Time Element

In researching this book, I asked sponsorees what they found to be the most difficult aspect of finding sponsorship. Most people who had to actively seek sponsorship answered with, "approaching prospective sponsors."

This may seem to be a surprising response considering the source – top equestrians, a number of whom have competed at the highest levels with crowds of people scrutinizing their performances. Even the most self-confident riders found approaching sponsors intimidating.

Much of the information contained in this book is about how to find sponsorship. But it's equally important to address the barriers that prevent riders from finding sponsorship.

### ■ ■ ■ The Lack of Self-Confidence Trap

It is common for riders seeking sponsorship to have self-doubts and to feel intimidated about asking individuals or corporations for money. Sponsorees indicated that the problem was one of being able to project self-confidence.

One well-known rider explains her solution for conquering the lack of self-confidence trap. "A few years ago I saw an interview of a famous actress who had starred in a Hitchcock film. She was having a particularly difficult time expressing the emotion needed in one scene. When she asked Hitchcock what to do about it, he told her, 'fake it.' That is what I do when I feel my self-confidence ebbing; I fake it, and it works. I focus on all of my positive attributes and, inevitably, I'm fine and able to make my request with confidence."

### ■ ■ ■ The "If Only" Syndrome

Another trap to avoid is the If Only syndrome. "If only I had better pictures to send a sponsor," or "If only I had a better video," or "If only I had more year-end awards to impress a sponsor with." These are all self-defeating thoughts that will prevent you from achieving your goal of finding a sponsor.

Push these thoughts out of your mind and focus on your goal and what you do have to offer a sponsor. And, if necessary, improve what you can – the pictures and the video!

### ■ ■ ■ The Do Nothing Pitfall

Finally, to guarantee that you won't find a sponsor, stay home and do nothing except think of all the *If only* scenarios and all the reasons why a sponsor should help someone else.

Or, develop a proposal, call people, write people, and get out there and actively promote yourself. The 10, 50, 100, or however many no's will be meaningless when you get that single yes.

### ■ ■ ■ When No Isn't Necessarily No

It is important to understand that a negative response will occasionally turn into a positive response at a future time. You may have approached a prospective sponsor at an inopportune moment. Either it is not financially feasible for this person to help you at this time or they are preoccupied with other activities. Here you have to use your own judgment to determine if this person might help you at some later date, and then make a note to yourself to approach them again in the future.

Listen carefully to people's reasons for not funding your efforts. Possibly your plan needs revision, or you need to ask for different things from different people. As you will see in the following chapters, most sponsorees have found several sponsors to provide them with different types and levels of sponsorship. Any help is going to get you closer to your goal: don't hold out for a single sponsor to handle 100% of your needs. Your chances are greatly improved by approaching different people for different things.

## ■ ■ ■ Helpful Hints from Sponsorees

Successful sponsorees offered the following advice: maintain a positive attitude and persevere. There will inevitably be discouraging moments – sometimes a string of them – but you can't let this stop you. Contact potential sponsors when you are feeling energetic and can present yourself to your best advantage. Soliciting sponsorship is challenging under the best of circumstances; you don't want the added burden of being tired or stressed from a difficult day at work.

Finally, those sponsored emphasized that being shy won't get you anywhere. You have to be very forthright in explaining your plan and asking for assistance, and with corporate sponsors, it is imperative that you state how *they* will benefit from investing in *you.*

## ■ ■ ■ How Long Does It Take To Find Sponsorship

For people who had sponsorships offered to them without ever looking, no time at all!

However, for people who had to actively pursue sponsors – which was the majority – there was a lot of variation in the amount of time it took to find sponsorship. Some people were able to find sponsorship in less than six months while others "spent years looking." Time disparities are caused by a number of things: the dedication with which people sought sponsorship, the amounts sought, the revision of proposals to specifically meet the needs of a particular sponsor, learning better techniques for approaching sponsors, and learning to approach the right people or companies.

Very few of the sponsorees interviewed received everything they needed from a single sponsor. Most had sponsorships of varying sizes with different people and organizations. Almost all sponsorees brought something into the sponsorship with them. Either tangibles such as a horse, equipment, or a training facility, or else the ability to train and compete the horse and a promise to promote the sponsor's products.

# The Sponsored Riders

# Newspaper Article Secures
# Grand Prix Horse
# for Michelle Gibson

### ■ ■ ■ Profile

Michelle Gibson began riding at age six and at 16 rode in a clinic conducted by Michael Poulin, Grand Prix rider/trainer who was on the 1992 Olympic Bronze Medal Dressage Team. Accepting Poulin's offer to take a position as a working student, Michelle moved from her Roswell, Georgia home to Fairfield, Maine with her Trakehner mare, Chaussee. Eighteen months later, 20-year-old Michelle made the courageous step of moving to Germany to train with Willi Shultheis and Rudolf Zeilinger. For six years, Michelle has filled the role of working student and star pupil, working six- and seven-day weeks and riding seven to ten horses per day.

While competing in Germany in 1995, Michelle received the Best Seat Award twice, posted the two highest scores ever posted by an American rider, and rode Peron to be Germany's number one money-winner for the year. In addition, Michelle received her German Riding License at the Grand Prix level (which is rarely given to a non-German), was named the U.S. Olympic Committee's Female Equestrian of the Year, was nominated for the U.S. Olympic Committee's Female Athlete of the Year, was one of five riders from all disciplines nominated for the Hertz/American Horse Shows Association Equestrian of the Year, and was the only American rider listed among the top 20 dressage riders in the world by the Federation Equestre Internationale.

## ■ ■ ■ The Olympic Quest

Many riders dream the Olympic dream, but only a few have the talent or determination to attain this goal. Michelle Gibson is one of the few and she pursues her goal with dedication and single-mindedness. Even though Michelle does not have vast financial resources of her own, her efforts led her to her goal of representing the U.S. in the 1996 Olympic Games.

As Michelle's riding education caught up with her innate talent, it became apparent to dressage experts in Germany and the U.S. that Michelle had all the right ingredients to become an Olympic team member. However, the lack of a horse and sufficient funds were ever-present problems.

In 1993, Michelle and her parents created a portfolio in an effort to raise the money necessary to purchase an international quality horse for Michelle. The 31-page portfolio included a resume, articles, testimonials, photographs, and a plan and budget that would take Michelle through the 1996 Olympic Games. Numerous proposals were sent to corporations but with disappointing results. Michelle refused to be discouraged and continued to pursue her training with energy and determination.

## ■ ■ ■ *The Atlanta Journal & Constitution* Profiles Michelle

Michelle's positive attitude prevailed and she got her big break shortly after being written up in *The Atlanta Journal & Constitution* as a local athlete with an Olympic dream – a big, expensive, Olympic dream. The article profiled Michelle and specifically described her equine and financial needs. Fortuitously, the article crossed the desk of Russell Webster whose wife, Carole Meyer-Webster, owns the Grand Prix Trakehner stallion, Peron. Russell was intrigued by the article and faxed it to Carole in Tennessee where she works as a radiologist.

Carole was interested and the Meyer-Websters invited Michelle to visit their Hidden Springs Farm in Lafayette, Georgia to ride Peron. The meeting went well by everyone's account. Russell describes the meeting: "Her family came with her. They are a very nice family and very supportive of their daugh-

Karl-Heinz Frieler photo

*"It's blood, sweat, and tears every day," says Olympic dressage rider Michelle Gibson. "Nobody bothered to tell me how expensive it was; not that it mattered. I probably would have done it anyway."*

ter. There is a lot of love and respect. Michelle is well qualified to work with Peron, and she has good values." Although Michelle and the Meyer-Websters were complete strangers before Michelle's partnership with Peron, they have developed a strong friendship and have never had a formal written agreement. The Meyer-Websters are among the few remaining from the 'old school' who believe that your word is your bond.

The Meyer-Websters solved Michelle's problem of the right horse for her goal. They also pay veterinary, blacksmith, and tack expenses. Michelle is a working student for Rudolf Zeilinger in Germany and pays her training expenses in this way. Most of her competitions are financed by the money she wins competing.

## ■ ■ ■ Scholarships, Sponsorships, and Newsletter Keep Michelle On Track

Michelle has secured different types of assistance during the past few years. In 1993, Michelle applied for and was awarded a training grant from the Carl-Heinrich Asmis Foundation. And, while living in Georgia, Michelle approached Brad and Laura Thatcher, owners of Applewood Farm in Alpharetta, to provide board for Peron at no charge and they obliged. In addition, the Thatchers hosted two fundraising picnics to benefit Michelle.

"We tried many times and sent out portfolios in an effort to get sponsorship for Michelle," says Michelle's mother, Marie. "After years of struggling, we began to get help from the places we least expected, none of which were large corporations." A family at the barn where Michelle was boarding came up with the first donation, which sent Michelle and Peron to New Jersey to a clinic with Zeilinger." Additionally, several friends in Georgia have repeatedly come through and proffered different levels of financial support for Michelle.

Marie sends a newsletter to people who have supported or are currently supporting Michelle's efforts. She brings them up to date on Michelle's activities, her competition results, and her plans for the future. "The newsletter has proved to be very important. It is a means for keeping people interested and for reporting Michelle's results so that they know she is consistently performing well."

## ■ ■ ■ Fundraiser Builds Hopes and Bank Account

In May of 1996, Brad and Laura Thatcher came to Michelle's assistance once again by hosting a fundraiser for her at their farm. They sent out invitations, provided a catered lunch, showed videos of Michelle and Peron performing, and had riders perform jumping and dressage demonstrations. The attendance was excellent and attendees proved their excitement regarding Michelle's Olympic Team prospects by making generous contributions. Those who could not attend were equally generous in mailing donations. "In spite of terrible weather with pouring rain, everyone had a wonderful time," says Marie.

## ■■■ It Gets Easier Coming Into the Home Stretch

After enormous struggles to raise money, the six months prior to the 1996 Olympic Games were finally a time that Michelle could focus 100% of her attention on riding and training and no longer worry about money issues.

Marie says that a number of events came together that enabled Michelle to concentrate on her riding. Among them were the numerous equine journals that published articles about Michelle's and Peron's outstanding achievements against the best European riders. Marie felt that the "Road to Atlanta" series done by *The Chronicle of the Horse* was especially beneficial in bringing Michelle to the attention of the equine community.

In addition, Karen Reid, owner of Foxfire Farm in Fox Island, WA, had met Michelle through a friend and was determined to help Michelle and Peron get back to the U.S. for the Final Selection Trials. She ran an ad in *The Chronicle of the Horse* auctioning a breeding to her stallion, Linaro, with the proceeds to go to the Michelle Gibson and Peron Sponsorship Fund. Karen was gratified by the number of people who made bids and was able to mail Michelle a check for $1,650.

The problem of transporting Michelle, Peron, and their entourage back to the U.S. for the final selection trials was solved by Service Guido Klatte and the Dutta Corporation, both international horse transporters. Klatte agreed to transport Michelle and Peron to New York, and Tim Dutta agreed to provide all of the transportation within the U.S. – all at no charge. Klatte also provided airfare for Rudolf Zeilinger, Zeilinger's wife, and Peron's groom.

It was gratifying for the Gibsons to also have the support of the American Trakehner Association (ATA). The ATA formed a fund for Michelle that was administered by The Dressage Foundation, Inc. Donations made through The Dressage Foundation, Inc. are tax deductible. In the final months, the U.S. Olympic Committee provided a grant to Michelle as well.

### ■ ■ ■ The Meyer-Websters' Perspective

When the Meyer-Websters were asked why they decided to sponsor a rider, Russell Webster answers, "Our goal was to get our horse to the Olympics. We are not going into the business of building a base of riders, but if we had another horse of the same caliber and met a rider as dedicated as Michelle, then we would consider another sponsorship situation. Riders like Michelle deserve to have a chance."

The Meyer-Websters are pleased with the partnership of Peron and Michelle and feel that they have benefited by this relationship. "We have had the satisfaction of seeing a top rider reach her goals and our horse reach his full potential," says Russell.

### ■ ■ ■ Summary

Although every step of the way has been a financial challenge for Michelle, she has persevered and found a variety of sponsorships to make her Olympic dream a reality. As Marie says, "It came together because she hung in there a long time, and she performed well consistently. Sponsorship requires a great deal of flexibility, persistence, and hard work. You have to show people that you can do what you said you would do and prove that you are for real."

With an individual fifth at the 1996 Olympic games and a team bronze medal, Michelle has proved beyond doubt that she is "for real."

# Debbie Shaffner Stephens Asks "What Can I Do For My Sponsor?"

## ■ ■ ■ Profile

An Illinois native and University of Syracuse graduate with a degree in Sociology, Debbie Shaffner Stephens has turned her riding hobby into a very successful career.

Debbie works out of her Centennial Farm in Glenmoore, Pennsylvania. With co-trainer Heidi Earle, she has built Centennial Farm into one of the most successful show barns in the U.S. Debbie has a keen eye for selecting talented young horses and turning them into winners. She has helped develop such greats as Conrad Homfeld's Abdullah, Debbie Dolan's Grand Prix champion VIP, Hiro Tomizawa's World Championship mount Don Carlos, and many others.

In April 1991, Debbie placed seventh on Volan in the Volvo World Cup Finals, tying with Anne Kursinski as the highest-placing American riders. When Volan was unable to compete in the Pan American Games selection trials, Debbie competed on Poor Richard who was just entering Grand Prix competition and they qualified. They went to Havana, Cuba and helped the U.S. win the Team Bronze Medal. In 1991, *L'Annee Hippique* rated Debbie as the Second Best Woman Grand Prix Jumper Rider in the world.

In 1992, Debbie was the second alternate on the USET Olympic Show Jumping Team with Texas T, and in 1993, she was once again on *L'Annee Hippique's* list of the top 20 riders in the world. In the same year, she rode away with the American Grand Prix Association (AGA) championship. Beside these impressive results, Debbie has also driven away from competitions in new cars: a BMW for her 1982 high jump record, a Cadillac for her 1992 AGA win, and a Lancia for being the leading rider in Rome.

In 1995, Debbie qualified for the Pan Am Team and traveled to Buenos Aires, Argentina where she helped the U.S. secure the bronze medal in the Nations Cup. Debbie is currently competing Pacifica and Timings Right at the Grand Prix level.

### ■ ■ ■ Aiming High

Debbie Shaffner Stephens has been aiming high since age 10 when she competed at Madison Square Garden in the Regular Working Hunter Division. Her career has been a long series of successes, including tying with Dennis Murphy for an outdoor high jump record of 7'8" in 1982 aboard Spindletop Rocky Raccoon.

With goals that require a lot of money as well as a lot of talent, Debbie has had to be resourceful and seek outside financial assistance. This sent Debbie in search of potential sponsors.

### ■ ■ ■ It Takes Time to Find Sponsorship

Although "it took years and years to get sponsorship," explains Debbie, she now has the support of Miller Harness Company, Nutramax Corporation (manufacturer of Cosequin), and an anonymous corporate sponsor. She actively sought sponsorship, but was adamant about representing only companies whose products she believes in and uses herself.

Because there is not much television coverage of horse sports, Debbie initially found it difficult to find a sponsor. Her focus was on demonstrating that she could keep a potential sponsor's name prominently displayed by consistently placing well and by her willingness to promote their products.

A combination of factors led to Debbie's finding sponsorship: "A successful competition record, being in the right place at the right time, and approaching potential sponsors," she says. Debbie's sponsorship proposal included her

James Leslie Parker photo

*"The high point of my experience with a sponsor is when they feel they have gotten their money's worth from sponsoring me," says Grand Prix jumper rider Debbie Shaffner Stephens.*

resume, competition record, photographs, a video, budget, and letters of recommendation.

Debbie says that her sponsors' goals are "to get exposure and to sell their products. It is my responsibility to promote the sponsor's product at every possible opportunity. The biggest challenges are exposure of their product and winning."

All three sponsors provide Debbie with their products and cover some of her expenses including board, competition expenses, and transportation.

## ■ ■ ■ The Horses

The sponsoree's ownership of horses is not a prerequisite to a successful sponsorship agreement. Debbie owns some of the horses she competes, while others are owned by clients. She finds that this works well for her. Some of the horses are insured, but insurance issues are handled by the owners.

## ■ ■ ■ Non-Equestrian Sponsors Versus Equestrian Sponsors

In the past, Debbie has had some sponsors who were not horse people and this was sometimes difficult. "If they were [horse people], they would have had a better understanding of how hard this business is," explains Debbie. She has appreciated all of the help she has received along the way and especially enjoys her three current sponsors who are all knowledgeable about the vicissitudes of the horse business.

## ■ ■ ■ Why Sponsors Select Debbie

As John Craven, International Wholesaler and Sponsorship Specialist for Miller Harness Company says, "Debbie Stephens certainly has a phenomenal success record which has not been limited to one or two horses. Debbie has been a pro for a number of years and has found and developed a number of horses to the Grand Prix level. She has proven herself over time.

"She is wonderfully social, very gracious, and willing to talk to spectators, children, and amateurs," continues Craven. "She gives back as much as anyone who is a sponsored rider, and these people have limited time. She is a wonderful emissary for us, and she has the desire to give back to the industry."

As for the personal quality that Debbie feels is most important to her sponsors, "It is my attitude of *what can I do for them*, rather than *what can they do for me*.

"Winning the AGA championship and the American Invitational (both in 1993) are the accomplishments that I think have been the most significant to my sponsors," she says. "These competitions are the 'crown jewels' of show jumping, however, the high point of my experience with a sponsor is when they feel they have gotten their money's worth from sponsoring me."

"What can I do for my sponsor" is Debbie Shaffner Stephens' motto, and it has proved to be a good one. Because Debbie is always looking for ways to showcase her sponsors' products, she now has three corporate sponsors. They not only appreciate Debbie's skill as a horsewoman and spokesperson, but they also know that she will go the extra distance for them and seek ways to enhance their image and visibility.

# Marindi Coward Thinks and Acts Creatively to Find Sponsorship

### ■ ■ ■ Profile

Marindi Coward and her husband Mick are involved in the horse business at their 17-acre Lone Pine Ranch in Pocatello, Idaho. Mick is a farrier and Marindi teaches riding, trains horses, and trains owners how to train their horses. They stand an AQHA stallion and are gradually expanding their facility and their services.

Marindi became interested in horses as a small child, but was unable to pursue riding due to constant moves necessitated by her father's job with the Army. Finally, in 1976, her family settled in Idaho, and Marindi, then 12-years-old, was able to purchase her first horse. This horse was green-broke, so Marindi received her initial riding education through books, her uncle, her involvement in a 4-H club, and hands-on experience. After high school, Marindi had to sell her horse and didn't ride for almost three years until she met her husband who had two pleasure horses.

With their mutual interest in horses, it was only natural that they should decide to go into the horse business. Mick went to farrier school in 1992 and

1993, and Marindi rode in her first clinic with well-known rider/trainer John Lyons in 1993. Since then they have worked as a team to increase their equine knowledge and build their horse business.

## ■ ■ ■ A Career Goal Drives Marindi Coward

After riding in one of John Lyons' clinics and auditing five more, Marindi was certain that she wanted to sign up for his certification program. Marindi paid her way to participate in the five clinics by working in John's trade booth. In May of 1995, Marindi officially enrolled in Lyons' certification program.

The John Lyons certification program is an intensive series of ten five-day sessions spread over 18 months. The tuition is $15,000 and each participant is responsible for bringing two untrained horses with them. The tuition does not cover transportation for horses or student, horse board, meals, or incidentals. The program is a significant commitment of time, energy, and money – but this did not deter Marindi. She knew it was the right program for her for two reasons: she was anxious to learn John's techniques, and she felt that certification through his program would be beneficial to her horse business.

## ■ ■ ■ Overcoming Obstacles

Finding the necessary cash for Marindi to enroll in the John Lyons program was a challenge for Mick and Marindi. They discussed the program at length, devising plans for how she could attend without jeopardizing them financially. With careful planning, ingenuity, and the Cowards' strong commitment to their horse business, they were able to make it all come together.

Marindi set about calculating how much money she would need, how she would raise it, and how she would acquire two horses suitable for the program. From the time she decided to enroll in November 1994 until the program start date in May 1995, Marindi developed some creative plans for securing financial assistance.

A $3,000 deposit is required by the program upon registration. Marindi's mother-in-law of St. James, NY, a horse enthusiast, agreed to pay the deposit if Marindi would agree to come to New York and do a clinic or a demo after completing the program. That got Marindi over the first hurdle.

Marindi did not even have one horse that fit the program's requirements, so the next hurdle was to get two horses. The first horse was offered by a friend who also agreed to provide Marindi with $5,000 in cash to put toward the tuition. The horse would be trained in the program, and Marindi would share her knowledge and training with the owner upon her return. The next horse

Mick Coward photo

*"My way is not the only way," says Marindi Coward regarding her approach to finding sponsorship, but her success rate proves that it is a good way.*

came from the man who delivers hay to Marindi's farm. He had a seven-year-old AQHA mare that was completely untrained. The horse did not fit in with his plans, so he was happy to sell her for only $400 to someone who would do well by her. With the horse situation settled, there were still the issues of transportation and the cash balance needed to pay for the program.

Marindi's husband Mick creatively solved the transportation problem by offering to shoe a client's horses for 18 months in exchange for the use of their trailer.

Marindi still needed the cash to pay the balance of the tuition and expenses beyond tuition. She contacted everyone she could think of who was familiar with John Lyons either firsthand or by reputation. Donors contributed $2,000 total with the agreement that Marindi would share her knowledge with them on a one-to-one basis.

"I spend a week at a time in the program," says Marindi, "I take extensive notes, type them up, and give them to my sponsors. Then I teach them using my own horse or their horse. I help them until they thoroughly understand the particular lesson. This gives me the opportunity to become secure in the knowledge that I have gained, and their feedback is a chance for me to find out if I am explaining things clearly. I will be giving clinics and having them videotaped so that I can see where I need improvement. I hope to have John review and critique them as well. I have come across a lot of people who want to send their horses for training. If there had been more time between when I decided to do the program and when it started, I could have raised a lot more money."

## ■ ■ ■ Creativity — Marindi's Hallmark

Marindi was committed to the program, confident in her ability to raise the money she needed, and creative in finding ways to make everything come together to her satisfaction. Although Marindi came up with what she needed, she had two interesting ideas beyond those described above.

The first idea involved approaching the local tack shop and requesting financial assistance to attend the Lyons program. She talked to them about carrying John Lyons' products – books, videos, round pens, headstalls, etc. – and offered to be in the shop on specific dates to discuss these products and answer customers' questions. She also offered to do a demonstration. She pointed out to the store manager that he could simultaneously increase his inventory by carrying John Lyons' products *and* be a John Lyons dealer in the area. The tack store was willing to offer Marindi a trainer's discount once she became certified, but was not willing to make a commitment beyond that. However, Marindi was not discouraged by their response and still feels that it was a viable plan. She has not pursued this route because other tack stores are too far away for her to be able to make the same offer that she made to her local tack store.

Marindi has a good idea for people with horse transportation problems. She suggests asking a trailer manufacturer for the loan of a trailer. The manufacturer could paint appropriate signage on the side of the trailer proclaiming their sponsorship, thereby increasing buyers' awareness of their product. If you are traveling a great deal, this is a lot of free advertising for a trailer manufacturer.

As well as being creative and hardworking in her fundraising efforts, Marindi exudes a nice combination of confidence and humility regarding her training techniques. "My attitude is that my way is not the only way."

Although Marindi says that her fundraising methods may not be ideal for everyone, they certainly have been successful for her and they highlight the importance of thinking creatively when developing strategies for securing sponsorship.

# Donald V. Little Jr. Espouses the Value of Networking

## ■ ■ ■ Profile

Polo player Donald V. Little Jr. resides in Ipswich, Massachusetts with his wife, Holly. Holly shares Don's interest in horses and is actively involved in keeping their polo ponies fit.

Don was riding before he could walk and learned to ride in Pony Club before discovering polo at age nine. He played in his first polo tournament at 12 years of age. Since he is from a family of polo players (Don's father, grandfather, uncle, and several cousins all play polo), Don didn't have to look far for inspiration or for training.

Through his father, Donald V. Little Sr., and Dave Roberts, now the Assistant Manager of the Gulfstream Polo Club in Florida, Don received most of his polo training. He supplemented his education by attending clinics – including a week-long clinic at Yale – and by working on a ranch in Argentina for six months when he was 20 years old. While the majority of polo players are rated as two goal or lower out of a possible 10, Don is rated as a four goal outdoor player and a six goal indoor player. Don has played up and down the east coast as well as in England, France, and Argentina.

Don is President of Centennial Farms and works full time syndicating racehorses from his Boston, Massachusetts office. Centennial Farms has produced numerous stakes winners including 1992 Sprint Champion and Eclipse Award Winner, Rubiano, and 1993 Belmont Stakes Winner, Colonial Affair. While Don's career is with racehorses, his serious hobby is polo.

## ■ ■ ■ The Expense of Pursuing Polo

Polo is one of the more expensive horse sports and, to be competitive, a player needs at least four horses – seven to eight are ideal. Not only is the upkeep of this many horses costly, but it usually requires the added expense of a full-time groom. Tournament fees are high, and there is very little in the way of prize money to offset any of these expenses. (The only significant purse in the U.S. is a $100,000 tournament held each year at the Royal Palm Polo Club in Boca Raton, FL.)

The average entry fee for a local tournament is $500 per team, while a tournament such as the U.S. Open costs $15,000 per team. To compete in tournaments, polo players must be members of the U.S. Polo Association and pay an annual membership fee of $125. Additionally, there are grounds fees for riders who are associated with a polo club.

Regarding finding sponsors, Don says, "In some cases I have actively sought sponsors, and in other instances, they have sought me. All of my sponsors have been found by *networking;* word of mouth and phone calls. I have never made any formal written requests for sponsorship." Past sponsors include Revlon, Glenlivet, and Range Rover.

Don seeks sponsorships for one-year time frames. Sponsorships are for one year because ratings of players change annually, so different teams are formed for that tournament schedule. "Sponsorship enables me to keep playing the sport I love," says Donald V. Little Jr. For the past five years, Don has had a different sponsor each year. In 1996, Don's sponsor was the Boston Polo Team captained by Michael Bucci.

## ■ ■ ■ The Sponsorship Relationship

Sponsors of Don's tend to be friends or teammates. He explains the relationship, "They don't expect any type of financial return from their sponsorship, and I don't have any written agreements with them. They expect me to play hard and perform at my maximum potential. They want to be part of a winning

Tom Stearns photo

*"Sponsorship enables me to keep playing the sport I love," says polo player Donald V. Little, Jr. "All of my sponsors have been found by networking: word of mouth and phone calls."*

team. They are looking for people who are honest, personable, and try hard. They also want my coaching."

For Don, the two biggest challenges relating to sponsorships are "finding people who want to part with enough money to cover all of my expenses and keeping sponsors happy by winning on a regular basis."

## ■ ■ ■ Budgeting

Expenses that Don's sponsors cover include tournament fees, upkeep of horses, grooms' expenses, and annual grounds fees. Don provides his own horses. He usually has seven or eight and takes all of them to each tournament. "This allows me to rotate my horses between chukkers [there are six chukkers (segments) in a game] so that they stay fresh. When it comes down to the wire, the same horse may be used for two chukkers," explains Don.

"The most important budget item to account for is enough money to pay for proper help because the horses are the most important aspect of polo and their health and well-being are vital to the results," says Don. "It is beneficial to have sponsors who are hands-on horse people because they understand this. They also appreciate my ability and realize that I can help them improve their game."

Saving money where possible is important too. Although Don does have one homebred in his current string of horses, he says that this is a much more expensive way of doing it. He recommends purchasing three- or four-year-old Thoroughbreds off the track.

## ■ ■ ■ Don's Advice to Riders Looking for Sponsors

Once you have the training and experience, Don's advice for riders looking for sponsorship is, "Networking." And, once you have sponsorship, "always give 100% on the playing field, be honest, and be able to teach."

# Mark Leone is Sponsored by Italian and Canadian Companies

## ■ ■ ■ Profile

Mark Leone and his two brothers, Armand and Peter, have been involved with horses since childhood. Their parents started Ri-Arm Farm in Oakland, New Jersey, which Mark now operates. The Leones got started with Welsh ponies, which they rode and drove.

As the Leone brothers got older and developed as riders, they focused on competing in the jumper ranks. Although Mark has tried two other careers – real estate and travel work for a lumber company – he was lured back to the horse business in 1989. He is completely immersed in horses and rides, competes, teaches, trains, buys, sells, gives clinics, and boards and breeds horses at his 34-stall facility.

Mark has always taken his riding very seriously and trained with George Morris for five years and with Michael Matz for two years. He has benefitted by riding with some top European trainers as well. Mark's goal was to become a well-rounded, knowledgeable horseman.

At Ri-Arm Farm, Mark offers a broad range of instruction: show hunters and equitation for young riders, adult riders, and jumpers; however, Mark says that his preference and main thrust is jumpers. He has been breeding horses since the mid-eighties and buys and imports horses in the hopes of producing Grand Prix jumpers. Ri-Arm currently stands the stallion Loro Piana Artos, who was purchased as a yearling and developed into a Grand Prix horse.

### ■ ■ ■ The Team Leone Concept

Because it typically costs between $40,000-$50,000 per year to campaign a single Grand Prix jumper, Mark Leone and his brothers realized they would need to find additional financial backing to pursue their show jumping goals.

"The idea of getting a sponsor initially developed in 1984 when Armand, Peter, and I really started competing at Grand Prix," says Mark. The Leones recognized and capitalized on their uniqueness as a family team. "We had some international background and came up with the *Team Leone* concept. My brothers and I and one other rider competed as Team Leone in the AGA Team Championships in Florida in 1985. The total purse was $225,000 and the competition was spread over three days. Our team won the event, and it was televised on CBS Sports in January, 1986."

With the Team Leone concept formulated, Mark's brother, Peter, approached his employer, Merrill Lynch, for sponsorship of an evening of competition. Merrill Lynch agreed and the Leones had their first sponsorship experience.

### ■ ■ ■ The Crown Royal Experience

Armed with the confidence that they had something unique and marketable to offer a sponsor, the Leones were ready to move forward. Through a friend, they contacted the liquor company Crown Royal. The idea of Team Leone was fresh and captured Crown Royal's interest. In 1989 they became the Leones' sponsor. From 1989 to 1995, Mark enjoyed thrilling successes and was in a position to be a real presence for Crown Royal.

"Because Crown Royal is a liquor company, they have certain restrictions placed on them regarding advertising. They have to find ways to promote their products to the right market," says Mark. Crown Royal gets exposure not only by sponsoring Mark, but also by sponsoring Grand Prix competitions, and by having their name on a banner displayed on the arena wall of those competitions.

Mark goes on to say, "Crown Royal decided to sponsor events based on region – where they were strong and where they wanted additional promotion

John Neely photo

*Mark Leone performing a half hour meet and greet session in the Loro Piana Shop at the Hampton Classic Horse Show before he rode in the $100,000 Crown Royal Grand Prix presented by Loro Piana.*

of their product. We went to L.A., Hollywood, Dallas, Chicago, Memphis, Palm Beach, Southampton. They jockeyed around with various locations over the six years.

"During the Crown Royal sponsorship I must have won nine or ten of their events over a six year span, and I have won the rider title three out of six years. It was important to do well for them."

### ■ ■ ■ Ing. Loro Piana & C. Seeks Out Mark Leone

Toward the end of 1994, a new opportunity was in the offing for Mark. "I had just won the series, the finale, and it had been a good year for all of us," says Mark. "It was at this point that I became acquainted with the Italian-based textile firm of Ing. Loro Piana & C. (henceforth, Loro Piana) through Karen Powell, Executive Vice President of The Pinewood Corporation. It was very interesting to be sought out by another company, and I felt that it might be good to make a move. I had started the Crown Royal sponsorship with my brothers and we really had done it all. I never could do any better in a Crown Royal situation." Thus, with the help of Karen Powell and The Pinewood Corporation (a New York and Toronto-based sports agent), a sponsorship agreement was formed between Mark Leone and Loro Piana.

Mark promotes Loro Piana by using a Loro Piana emblazoned saddle pad under his saddle, by wearing their riding coat that was handmade for him in Italy, by carrying their corporate colored (blue and yellow) whip, and by transporting his horses in a van with *Loro Piana Show Jumping Team* painted prominently on the side. His horses wear Loro Piana monogrammed sheets and blankets, and their tack stall at shows is in the Loro Piana motif. And, if you are interested in Loro Piana products, Mark will graciously stop and talk with you about them and is always wearing their clothing.

"My apparel from Loro Piana is just gorgeous," says Mark. "It is a pleasure to wear their clothes, and I wear them with a lot of pride."

### ■ ■ ■ The Life of a Sponsored Rider

Sponsorship can require a huge commitment of time and effort on the part of the sponsoree and enormous amounts of travel. Mark travels about 30 weeks per year.

"There is a lot of pressure. You don't want to disappoint your sponsor. You are very aware of performance and the pains and sorrows that go with it. We're all out there doing the best we can and hoping that the odds and the percentages come our way. But you are going to have your share of misfortune. To make it all come together is tough. But you get used to it and it gets to be fun dealing with it."

Sponsorship is not necessarily easy to find either. Mark says that it took Team Leone about a year and a half to find their first sponsor. The Leones have utilized the expertise of a sports agent and Mark is quick to credit Karen Powell for setting up the Loro Piana sponsorship.

When asked about the enormous travel time, the competition pressure, and the pressure to promote his sponsor's products, Mark responds, "It takes some effort, but in the big picture it's well worth it."

## ■ ■ ■ Media Coverage of Horse Sports

When asked about media coverage (and television coverage, in particular), Mark says, "Horse sports have major TV coverage in Europe, whereas in the U.S. it is way in the background and has very little coverage. Canada also gives equestrian sports much greater coverage. In Canada there is CBC, CTV – many Canadian networks televise horse sports. To get NBC, CBS, or ABC involved in televising horse sports is extremely difficult."

Mark goes on to say, "I'd like to see equestrian sports incorporate a few more types of people. It is quite an elitist sport in terms of what it costs to be a rider and what it costs to keep a horse. It's not like tennis, or other sports that are available to a much wider range of people. In Europe, it is a little more affordable; there are more riding clubs, and it is a heavily viewed sport."

## ■ ■ ■ Sponsorship Agreements

Mark Leone's sponsor pays on a per annum basis. There is a minimum number of events that Mark must compete in and a certain number must be televised. Both the sponsor's and the rider's expectations are written into the sponsorship agreement.

"The sponsor pays a lease fee on an annual basis so that they can get the name of the horse, which is typical in a sponsorship agreement," explains Mark. "It costs money to change the horse's name, and you need to be training and competing several horses because you need depth. You need to develop a team of horses because one could go lame."

### ■ ■ ■ Retaining Amateur Status

"One important aspect of our Crown Royal sponsorship was that my brothers and I retain our amateur status in order to be eligible to ride in certain competitions. We were able to do this with the help of the AHSA, which is our national federation. All sponsorship money is funneled through the AHSA for a small handling fee. There is no limit to the amount of money a rider can receive." [For more information on rules pertaining to sponsored riders, see the chapter entitled *Rules and Restrictions for Sponsored Riders.*]

Although cash contributions have to go through the AHSA, contributions of feed or equipment do not have to be reported. The AHSA keeps on file a copy of all written agreements between sponsors and sponsorees who choose to utilize the AHSA's services.

### ■ ■ ■ The Sponsored Rider's Persona

"There are a lot of things involved with a sponsorship. Not just the actual performance in the ring, but the image you project, your visibility, your support staff, and your attendance at certain functions," explains Mark. "You are reaching out to people whether they be the sponsors, their friends, employees, children, or whomever. You do your part to make it possible for them to come see the horses and to be a part of it. Some are afraid of the horses or don't have the time to be involved, while others do have the time and really appreciate it. Through competitions and social events, I develop a rapport with the group, the company.

"The corporate sponsor knows that you are out on the road a certain number of weeks per year, that you are participating in certain regions, and that you are going to reach a certain number of people. Some of the events are on TV and in a decent year you are going to have multiple interviews – on TV or in print. The sponsor develops a persona through you. Results are important."

### ■ ■ ■ Depth and Breadth is a Safeguard

Mark currently competes five horses – four at Grand Prix and one at Intermediate. "Not all of these horses go to every show because they have to be able to rest," says Mark "You are fighting nature, injuries. It is important to have depth, otherwise injuries and accidents can put you out of the competition altogether.

"1995 was a difficult year with three of my five horses being injured (one in a trucking accident). But I was still able to compete in Mexico and finish the season. It is important from the sponsor's point of view to have several horses because unfortunate things do happen. Horses get hurt or sick just like human athletes. That's why sponsors look to develop an individual who has several horses available."

## ■ ■ ■ Mark's Advice to Riders Seeking Sponsors

"To keep yourself on top of the sport you have to be developing and working with horses," explains Mark. "That's what I am always trying to do – keeping horses up and coming.

"Give a little time, a little effort. Pay attention and do the best you can. Be articulate and willing to put yourself out a little bit. I think there are sponsorship opportunities for other riders."

# Valerie Kanavy Demonstrates
# Team Spirit

## ■ ■ ■ Profile

As a self-described backyard amateur with very limited initial training, Valerie Kanavy has risen to the top of the endurance riding world and was the 1984 World Champion with her Arabian gelding Pieraz.

Valerie describes her background as being "from a large family without a lot of money. At 11 years old, I bought my first horse with my piggy bank savings. I don't know how my parents allowed me to do this because we did not live on a farm. I just sort of said I wanted a horse and was going to do this and they didn't know how to say no. I threw newspapers and babysat to pay the board."

With a lack of any formal riding education, Valerie did very little showing – "and not very successfully" – in her home state of Kansas. "I started out riding western, but mostly I rode bareback because it was such a pain in the neck trying to get the saddle on," explains Valerie. She describes her schooling as "picking people's brains and learning by doing and having to solve my own problems. I would ask people what they knew about certain things. My education was an informal, cumulative sort of thing."

When Valerie's family moved to Virginia, she became interested in foxhunting, did some point-to-point racing, and started learning how to prepare and condition a horse. It was at about this time that Valerie read about endurance riding and the Tevis Cup in California. This piqued her interest and gave her the idea of trying a local competitive ride. It was a book by Walter Farley that was instrumental in Valerie's selecting an Arab for herself.

To date, Valerie has the most successful record of any endurance rider in the Race of Champions by consistently placing in the top 10. This is a large competition that is held once a year at different locations in the U.S., and the horses must meet rigorous qualifications to participate. Valerie has also won several Arabian national titles. "Interestingly enough I have not competed in our national conferences," she says. "They have a point system and I haven't actually competed for their cup because you go from event to event and gather points. Instead, I prefer to choose certain events that I want to do well at."

Valerie has also been successful competing abroad and is now "starting to take dressage lessons and do some formal stuff." With the help of her daughter and one employee, Valerie has eight horses of her own in training. Training takes place from January to November with a break for the month of December. Although she has had many requests to train riders and horses, Valerie's own horses are a full-time commitment.

## ■ ■ ■ The International Endurance Scene

Endurance competitions have led Valerie to such far off places as South America, Australia, and Europe. She is one of the few U.S. endurance riders competing abroad and has some interesting insights regarding her international competitors. "South America is relatively junior in their endurance endeavors but they have tremendous participation. The Australians have been doing endurance for quite a long time and I think that they have some very exceptional horses and riders. They have some of the best horses I've ever seen. The French have demonstrated quite repeatedly that they are excellent endurance riders.

"The Europeans have become very competitive. They are very diverse with so many different countries and different breeds: Hanoverians, Dutch Warmbloods, Holsteiners, etc. But a lot of their efforts have been impeded by trying to do endurance with their particular breed, and that doesn't necessarily work; however, they are coming around and Europe does have many excellent horse people. More and more I see Arabians, which tend to dominate the sport,

*"There are some companies that have contributed highly into this sport," says 1984 World Champion endurance rider Valerie Kanavy. "For those people, I do a lot of promotional things for free."*

being ridden in Europe too. Years ago approximately 10% of the entries in an endurance event were Arabians. Now, 40 to 50% of the entries are Arabians.

"Owning a horse in Europe is very different from owning a horse in the U.S. For $300 you can purchase a horse in the U.S. and keep it in your backyard. In Europe there are many rules and regulations and zoning, and oftentimes you can't own a horse if you haven't been through some sort of school."

## ■ ■ ■ Finding Sponsors

"I have been sponsored for the past 10 years and the sponsors have approached me," answers Valerie when asked how she found sponsorship. "Since winning the World Championship, I have been approached by several different people. Sometimes it's easy and sometimes it's hard because I don't feel comfortable endorsing a product I don't necessarily use. I have been in this situation and just said no."

## ■ ■ ■ Sponsorship Specifics

"A lot of companies have given me a product because they want my opinion on it," explains Valerie. "Products include clothing, equipment, feed, and supplements. Patagonia manufactures some riding equipment but also regular, good clothing. Miller Harness provides me with equipment such as horse blankets, bits, bridles, and other things that I might use. In the past, sponsors have primarily been companies who wanted my opinion on a product or my help with introducing it. They quoted me and used pictures of me in their advertising. Sponsors are motivated to offer sponsorships because of the growth of endurance riding and the fact that it is another market that they can expand into."

Valerie's sponsors include Patagonia, Eisers, Running Bear Farms, Animal Packer, California Go the Distance, Ariat boots, Penfield Feeds, Buckeye Feeds, Marine Minerals, ABC Performance, V-Max Performance Technology, XL Performance, DC Ice Boots, Sharon Saare endurance saddles, Ulster boots and saddles, and others.

Patagonia originally approached Valerie to be part of their Pro Program, and she subsequently approached them on behalf of the endurance team. "If we were more sophisticated about asking, sponsors would probably do more for us," comments Valerie. "We are novices at this, and very appreciative of Patagonia's support over the last few years. They give the team products. Some of our sponsors have made donations directly to the USET.

"Penfield Feed gives feed to the endurance team, and Buckeye Feed has a new electrolyte that I am about to try out," says Valerie. "I think that it is going to be a wonderful product." Steve Rojek, President of Slypner Shoes, sponsored the team for the 1995 North American Championship by providing them with Slypner Shoes. Valerie says that the shoes are very nice and that Steve helped out because of his own personal interest in the endurance event.

## ■ ■ ■ Sponsorship Agreements

According to Valerie's contract with Miller Harness, she must wear a Miller's cap and jacket around camp. In exchange, Valerie receives a certain amount of their products per year. "In the past, I haven't had to do anything very formal to receive product," says Valerie. "All I've done is occasionally appear in an ad. Sponsors like the fact that I am using their product, which is an endorsement.

"I've never been given cash by my sponsors, only product. As of yet, I haven't had to go to any promotional events, but I recently discussed a sponsorship with a company that does want me to do a promotional event. They will pay my travel costs plus a flat fee for the day. I just negotiated a sponsorship program with Equitana, and they are going to give our national organization [the American Endurance Ride Conference - AERC] a boost. Many of the sponsorships I solicit benefit team riders or AERC rather than me individually. Often I don't even get the product. I will agree to do something for a company if they will donate a saddle or whatever to AERC.

"Endurance is kind of a blue collar backyard sport, so we haven't been very sophisticated about approaching sponsors. The most we have done is ask for trophies or prizes for our events, or for help funding the North American or World Championship team. But individually, a few people have successfully found sponsorship. One person's husband is the CEO of a running shoe company, and she has gotten quite a bit in the way of merchandise."

## ■ ■ ■ Media Coverage

"I have been written up in *The Chronicle of the Horse, Western Horseman, International Arabian Horse, Arabian Horse Express, Equus, Practical Horseman, Horse Illustrated,* and a lot of European magazines – some of them I can't even read," says Valerie.

"Endurance rides are sometimes televised. The International Arabian Horse Association has produced a couple of films on their national championship that were seen by millions of viewers. Endurance riding is avidly followed by the general public in foreign countries – as are all types of riding," says Valerie.

"I won an event in Holland and it was on the evening news in a number of European countries. The piece was about 20 minutes long and devoted to the event. It was included in the sports segment of the regular evening news.

"The USET did a tremendous job of covering the 1984 games and produced three videos – one of the films was nominated for a national sports award. The people who produced the film have been doing horse events for many years, and they said this was the highlight of their film career. This film has circulated around the U.S. and is very compelling. It has made me very well-known. When the film was done, the AERC had just come under the USET umbrella. Since the USET depends on the public to fund all of our team sports, the press coverage was very beneficial. The endurance event was the only gold medal the U.S. brought home."

## ■ ■ ■ Some of the Sponsors and What They Provide

Valerie has significant influence with sponsors as can be seen by her list of sponsors below. These sponsors have helped Valerie individually and some of them have contributed to endurance teams at her request.

- Running Bear Farm – endurance tack
- California Go the Distance – bridles and breast collars for the team
- Ariat Boots – riding boots
- Marine Minerals – human electrolytes as well as horse products
- ABC Performance – supplements for horses
- V-Max Performance Technology – heart monitor system and saddle pads
- XL or Excel – monitors to take the horse's temperature through an electrode in the saddle pad
- Miller Harness Company – blankets and miscellaneous equipment
- Patagonia – clothing

## ■ ■ ■ Summary

"At this point it is not necessary for me to pursue sponsors. Financially, we are okay. If we were having a difficult time perhaps it would shed a different light on it. It is really nice to have warm blankets from Miller Harness, and shipping boots and things. I think sponsorships are a special thing for people who are in need of outside assistance."

# Ruth Hogan-Poulsen
# Seeks Sponsorship Abroad

## ■■■ Profile

Ruth Hogan-Poulsen, her mother Jeannette Hogan, and their partner Kathie Moulton operate East Hill Farm in Plainfield, Vermont. They teach, train, compete, and board horses at their 130-acre, 28-stall facility. Ruth also imports Danish Warmbloods, and she travels throughout New England giving clinics and judging schooling shows and events.

Ruth grew up in Vermont and began riding at a young age. Before immersing herself in dressage, Ruth trained and competed in hunters, equitation, Medal/Maclay, and evented through preliminary level. At the University of Vermont, Ruth was a pre-vet and nutritional major and stayed involved with horses by working at a nearby barn. During this time she became acquainted with the 4-year-old Thoroughbred/Dutch Warmblood gelding, Valentino, whom she subsequently purchased, trained, and competed through Intermediare I.

Numerous top trainers have influenced Ruth's riding and training techniques. Local trainers include Volker Brommann, Dr. H. L. M. Van Schaik, Judi Shailor, and Ruth's partner, Kathie Moulton. Upon Ruth's 1988 graduation from the University of Vermont, she moved to Pennsylvania to apply to veterinary school. However, her equestrian interests proved more alluring than vet school, and she opted to pursue her dressage education instead. Winters were spent training with different people, and in the spring, Ruth always returned to East Hill to help Kathie and her mother run their riding program. Trainers who have influenced Ruth since college are Lorinda Lende, Ann Guptill, Olympian Robert Dover, and Jane Savoie. Ruth names Jane Savoie as her primary trainer.

Ruth currently devotes the warmer months to teaching and training in Vermont and heads south in the winter to compete on the Florida circuit with her Danish Warmblood gelding, Mastermind.

### ■ ■ ■ An Opportunity Disguised as a Setback

While working for Robert Dover and Jane Savoie during the winters of 1992 and 1993, Ruth was spotted by a woman who admired her riding and training abilities. This person wanted to partake in the enjoyment of part ownership of a good dressage horse and joined forces with Ruth to import a competition quality Danish Warmblood.

Although this sponsorship arrangement worked well for a time, unforeseen circumstances necessitated the termination of the agreement. This situation might have discouraged many people, but it served to help Ruth in her resolve to move forward with her riding career.

Ruth looks back on the experience positively and with gratitude. "I am thankful that I had this opportunity as I could not have bought this horse on my own. It also helped me to expand into another area – helping friends and students select suitable Danish Warmblood dressage prospects." This experience was also fortunate because it led to Ruth's meeting a Danish rider who suggested that Ruth seek sponsorship in Denmark.

### ■ ■ ■ Seeking Sponsorship in Denmark

Sponsorship opportunities for Americans are not limited to the borders of the United States, and ingenuity and resourcefulness led Ruth Hogan-Poulsen to seek corporate sponsorship in Denmark. Ruth's story proves the importance of keeping an open mind regarding possible sponsorship opportunities. Although one sponsorship door closed on Ruth, others opened. Not only did Ruth decide to seek sponsorship abroad, but she was also able to help several people find good horses, which is something she finds personally satisfying.

Because of Ruth's love of Danish Warmbloods and her knowledge of the

Con Hogan photo

*"Energy," is Ruth Hogan-Poulsen's answer when asked what advice she would give to riders seeking sponsorship. "Decide on what direction you want to go in and be relentless. Always be very upbeat."*

Danes' pride in their horses, she appealed to this in her presentations to potential sponsors. She was confident that she could interest Danish executives in sponsoring a Danish horse in America to promote their products.

Ruth started out by sending letters to 15 corporations describing her plan, her riding credentials, and her goals. Of course, there was the added challenge of composing the letter in both English and Danish without losing the full impact of her message. Approximately one year elapsed between the time that Ruth made her initial contact with corporate sponsors in Denmark until the time that she actually met with them to discuss her idea in more detail.

In the fall of 1995, Ruth and her husband made the trip to Denmark to meet face-to-face with the 12 company heads who had expressed interest in Ruth's plan. She requested the same amount from each company to put toward competition expenses. The plan would span a one year period and be renewable. In exchange for financial support, Ruth would promote her sponsors' product(s).

Ruth is currently working with several companies, including one company that sells horse-related products. There is strong interest among the companies, but the Danes have the same apprehensions as Americans – the limited spectatorship and TV coverage of horse sports in the U.S. This is an objection that is a challenge for many equestrians seeking sponsors.

### ■ ■ ■ Ruth's Special Horse Gains Her Valuable Media Attention

In 1994, Ruth and her American sponsor purchased Mastermind as a 3-year-old. Mastermind had been approved for breeding for one year, but did not pass the second year inspection. Mastermind's failure to be approved for breeding proved to be a source of controversy. Several of the riders who had ridden him during the testing noted that he was "hard in the mouth." Because Mastermind was not approved, his owners decided to sell him. Ruth was impressed with him and baffled by the remarks of his being hard in the mouth. Through asking questions and contacting several people, she discovered that he had had wolf teeth extracted two weeks prior to the stallion testing and still had stitches. Satisfied that the problem was not with Mastermind, Ruth agreed to purchase him. In his first year of competition, Mastermind won 19 of the 21 training and first level tests entered!

In April of 1995 a Danish magazine, whose title translates to Horse and Rider, did an article about Mastermind and commented, "It makes us wonder if we should have sold this wonderful horse to the U.S." Ruth's love of her Danish horse and his successful show record are key points in promoting this pair to Danish sponsors.

### ■■■ Ruth's Perspective on Corporate Sponsors

Ruth explains that corporate sponsors have entirely different motives than private sponsors for funding an equestrian sponsorship. They look for a capable rider with name recognition who will promote their products in the U.S. Ruth is willing to promote corporate sponsors by putting their name(s) on her trailer and saddle pad, having a banner displayed when stabling at shows, distributing promotional materials when appropriate, and doing her utmost to stay in the limelight to give these companies' products maximum exposure.

### ■■■ Asking the Tough Question

"Approaching sponsors is the most difficult part for me," says Ruth, echoing numerous other sponsored riders. Approaching people for money is difficult under the best of circumstances, but Ruth had the added challenges of having to travel a great distance, convincing corporations selling non-equine products that she could represent them capably, and coping with the language barrier. "It was a challenge coming up with a letter to entice sponsors, and I was nervous about meeting with corporate heads," Ruth says.

"Energy," is Ruth's answer when asked what advice she would give to riders seeking sponsorship. She goes on to say, "Decide on what direction you want to go in and be relentless. Talk to everyone about your goals and future dreams. Always be very upbeat."

### ■■■ Contracts

Ruth is adamant about having a written contract with her sponsors. In this way, it is clear what the sponsoree is offering his/her sponsor and what the sponsor is offering the sponsoree. Everyone's expectations are clearly stated at the outset thereby minimizing the chances for misunderstandings. "It is imperative to have well-defined goals and to put everything in writing," explains Ruth. "The agreement should be very businesslike and include all aspects of the arrangement including purchase price, expenses, insurance issues, resale, and any other factors that may be important. It is important to make sponsors aware of the risks involved with horses so that they are prepared should anything go wrong."

## ■ ■ ■ Traits that are Assets to Sponsored Riders

Ruth is a hard working, positive, and self-described "financially thrifty" individual who stresses the importance of integrity in the care and training of her horses and in the treatment of sponsors. "I am dedicated to keeping my sponsors' costs down," says Ruth, "and to promoting their products whenever possible."

When Ruth first found sponsorship she had good local name recognition and some regional recognition. She feels that she gained publicity by working with Robert Dover and schooling horses at his farm. This is where she was noticed by her first sponsor.

"Name recognition is very important to corporate sponsors," explains Ruth, "but not as important for individual sponsors." Ruth keeps copies of articles about Mastermind on hand and her portfolio of competition results up-to-date for any interested potential sponsors to review. Contacting potential sponsors, keeping Mastermind in top form, and constantly updating her portfolio ensure that Ruth is ready at a moment's notice to field questions, send information out, or show Mastermind to potential sponsors.

# Beezie Patton Projects
# the Right Image

## ■ ■ ■ Profile

Beezie Patton got a head start on her riding career thanks to her parents being in the business of buying and selling young horses at their Apple Ridge Stable in Mequon, Wisconsin. As a junior rider, Beezie competed show hunters, and in 1981, at age 17, she went to train with Mike Henneghan in New Jersey for her last year as a junior.

In 1982, Beezie entered Southern Seminary Junior College in Virginia where she would be able to keep up with her riding. Although Southern Seminary is well-known for its equine studies, Beezie chose the Liberal Arts program so that she could later transfer to a four-year college. Beezie won the National Intercollegiate Championship while attending Southern Seminary, and decided to train with Katie Monahan (now Prudent) after her freshman year. Although accepted to the University of Virginia as a junior, Beezie opted to accept Katie's offer to stay on as a working student. As Beezie says, "This is when my jumper career really began." With one horse of her own and as many of Stillmeadow Farm's as she could manage to ride, Beezie had no shortage of quality horses to gain experience on. "This was my first string of top quality horses and included Medrano, Trudeau, and Rascal, all of whom belonged to Stillmeadow," says Beezie. "Katie was extemely helpful not only in training me, but also in helping me get a job at Stillmeadow."

French Rapture and Northern Magic are horses that Beezie rode to significant wins. In 1993, Beezie rode French Rapture to 5th place at the World Cup Finals in Goteborg, Sweden, and she won a number of Grand Prix jumping classes aboard Northern Magic, who was also the leading money-winner in the U.S. for two years.

Beezie has ridden on a number of winning Nation's Cup Teams and competed throughout the U.S. and in Europe, Canada, and Mexico. In July of 1987, Beezie was offered and accepted a job training and competing for John Madden Sales, Inc. in Cazenovia, New York and has been there ever since. Beezie now has a number of up and coming jumpers along with Allan Shore's proven horse, Dynamite. Among the less experienced horses are John Holmes' Husker Du, Beezie's parents' horse Lands End, Allan Shore's Innocence, Herbert Kohler's Imaginario, and Rettina who Beezie owns in partnership with John Madden, Barbara Wolff, and Carol Thompson.

## ■ ■ ■ Setting Goals

Beezie Patton describes her goals as "building a string of top jumpers and competing in the Olympics and World Championships." Not too long ago, these may have seemed like unrealistic goals. Not because Beezie doesn't possess the requisite talent and training, but because of the expense involved in purchasing and competing a single top jumper, never mind "a string" of them. Thanks to several private sponsors, Beezie has been able to make a name for herself in Grand Prix jumping. Through her consistent Grand Prix wins, she has been able to garner a number of private and corporate sponsorships. Beval, Ltd. provides Beezie with clothing and equipment, Agway supplies feed to John Madden Sales barn, and Grand Prix provides Beezie with clothing.

In most cases, Beezie has been in the fortunate position of having sponsorships offered to her. She was approached by Mark Walter of Beval Ltd. to represent his company (see chapter entitled *Beval, Ltd. Sponsors Events and Individuals*). Mr. & Mrs. Steffen and Barbara Wolff are local private sponsors who own Cincinnati Red, winner of the 1996 Devon Grand Prix. Barb has been very supportive of Beezie's riding and, when she learned that Agway might be interested in sponsoring a rider, she did not hesitate to approach them on Beezie's behalf.

Cheryl Bender Photo

*"Get started with someone really good," advises Grand Prix jumper rider Beezie Patton. "Maintain a good image and always do what is right."*

Although Beezie has successfully broken into the world of international show jumping she says that she had only regional name recognition when she found her first sponsor. However, she believes that name recognition is a very important factor in getting corporate sponsorship.

## ■■■ Various Services for Various Sponsors

What Beezie offers her sponsors varies because of the different nature of each sponsor. For her private sponsors, she is providing them with the enjoyment of watching their horses training at home and winning at major competitions. For the corporate sponsors, it is the promotion of their products.

Beval has their name on Beezie's coolers, trunks, and saddle pads, and Agway has provided her with an elaborate tack room setup with four sides and an array of promotional posters on their feeds. "We also wear hats and shirts provided by our sponsors.

"We attend a few trade shows or exhibitions for Agway," says Beezie "and once or twice a year we appear at their display and have a scheduled talk or question and answer session about what we do, how we do it, and how we think Agway Feed helps us. Most of our promotion for Agway, Beval, and Grand Prix riding apparel is done at the shows."

## ■■■ Relationships and Responsibilities

Beezie says that sponsors are looking for people who "have a good reputation in the horse world, a nice demeanor, good training skills, ability, and winningness." Some of Beezie's sponsors are riders, and Beezie says this can be particularly beneficial because they understand the horse business. Such is the case of Barbara Wolff. "Although Barb is not competing herself at the present time, she does a nice job of riding and schooling her own horses.

"To keep sponsors interested, keep it fun," says Beezie. "And if anything goes wrong, be up front — don't hide things." Beezie says she has been very fortunate with no major catastrophes to any of the horses nor any serious career slumps. There is the occasional minor injury but nothing that has been problematic. She makes it clear to her sponsors that making money at this game is very tough. Beezie's private sponsors enjoy purchasing talented young prospects for Beezie to develop, while some also hope to resell the horse for a profit. However, most are primarily involved because they like it. Others find traveling the circuit, which frequently takes them abroad, to be very satisfying.

### ■ ■ ■ Taking Things in Stride

In December of 1995, one of Beezie's private sponsors, Mr. & Mrs. Herbert Kohler, purchased the Grand Prix jumper Imaginario so that Beezie would have a good horse on which to try out for the Olympic Team. "We were in the top ten until the second to last trial at Devon where Imaginario sustained a slight injury in the second round," says Beezie. Rather than being devastated by missing an opportunity to be on the 1996 Olympic Jumping Team, Beezie is very philosophical and shows her respect and appreciation for Imaginario by saying, "We really do not know him well enough yet to go to the Olympics, but I think we'll have a top quality horse in the future."

In addition to the Wolff's Cincinnati Red and the Kohler's Imaginario, Beezie is also training the Kohler's Zabet, whom she rode to victory in the 1994 Four-Year-Old Jumper Futurity.

### ■ ■ ■ Do What Is Right

Beezie's advice to people starting out, is "to get started with someone really good. Katie Monahan Prudent was very helpful in getting me going." Regarding sponsorships, she says, "Maintain a good image and always do what is right."

### ■ ■ ■ A Note from John Madden

When discussing Beezie's sponsorships with her employer John Madden, he strongly emphasizes the integral role that the private sponsors play not only in their support of Beezie as an individual, but in their support of the sport of show jumping as well. "The vast majority of [Beezie's sponsorship] money comes from private funds," says John, "and the reality is that the private sponsors do more than the corporate sponsors. All too frequently, they don't get the credit that they so well deserve.

"Last year we approached the Kohlers, who we didn't know all that well, and asked if they would be interested in purchasing a horse that Beezie could try out for the [1996 Olympic show jumping] team on. They gave us the go ahead to purchase Imaginario even though they knew it would be a long shot because of his age and lack of experience. He did not make the team but the Kohlers were very gracious and supportive throughout the selection trials and seemed to enjoy the process. And now we have a horse that is a good bet for the future – the World Championships and the next Olympics."

# Richard Rader's Friends Help Spread the Word

### ■ ■ ■ Profile

Born in Long Island, New York, Richard Rader moved to the Virgin Islands with his family at age 10 and, through his long residence there, is now a Virgin Islands citizen. In 1977 Richard returned to the United States to attend the University of Delaware where he was able to ride and train with Three-Day eventer Ralph Hill.

In 1984, Richard represented the Virgin Islands in the Olympic Three-Day event competition riding Peuce. Richard qualified for the Pan Am Games on Cestus in 1995, but importation requirements prevented them from competing.

After Richard's graduation from college in 1981, Richard and his wife purchased Sterling Hill Farm in North East, Maryland and started their own horse business. Richard rides, trains, teaches, and attends to the many details inherent with owning the farm while simultaneously vying for a spot on the 1996 Virgin Islands Three-Day Event Team.

Under Richard's capable guidance, his star performer is Dr. & Mrs. David Goodman's Trakehner stallion Cestus. Cestus has become a verifiable Advanced level Three-Day horse, having competed in 3 three-star events, and completing two of them.

## ■ ■ ■ Finding a Horse

With an eye toward the Olympics, Richard needed a very special horse, and just as importantly, he needed help in financing that horse. Richard's skill and determination impressed his friends and students who worked on his behalf in a number of ways to help him toward his Olympic goal. One student happened to be in a situation where she could assist Richard in finding the ideal horse. This person was speaking with Patricia (Pat) Goodman, owner of Wonderland Farms – a Trakehner breeding farm in Pennsylvania – and mentioned Richard's need. At the time, Pat was looking for a talented individual to bring along her promising stallion, Cestus.

As Pat says, "I was at the end of a long road of trying to find someone to whom to give the use of Cestus, and we could not afford to put him in training with anyone. I became acquainted with Richard through a client, who was training with him and had moved her horses to his facility. She knew he was in need of a good horse to hopefully take to the Olympics. Richard was needy enough to rise to the challenge, and I was very grateful to have him accept. Besides, I liked what I saw, and I trusted the opinion of our client that he was a solid citizen and a good rider."

The formidable task of obtaining a talented Three-Day horse was solved through Richard's making people aware of his needs. This ultimately led to his connecting with a person who was in a position to help.

## ■ ■ ■ Raising Money Through a Raffle

With Richard's goals being the 1995 Pan Am Games and the 1996 Olympics, he has had to put almost as much effort into fundraising as he has his training.

Richard developed the idea of raffling off a Virgin Islands vacation. Friends who own a resort in the Virgin Islands responded positively to Richard's request of donating a week's vacation with the raffle proceeds to go toward the expenses of sending Richard and Cestus to the Pan Am Games.

Tickets were sold for $50 each over a three month period and primarily through word of mouth and the kindness of friends and supporters. A total of 60 tickets were sold. Although the raffle did raise $3,000 for Richard, it was

Patricia L. Goodman photo

*Richard Rader says that it is who you know, either directly or indirectly, that count most when it comes to finding sponsorship.*

not as successful as he had hoped and did not raise enough money to cover all of his Games' expenses.

This raffle was Richard's first foray into fundraising. Although he did not achieve his goal of selling 200 tickets, he learned some valuable lessons from the experience. In retrospect, Richard believes the ticket price was too high. Of course, lowering the price would necessitate selling a lot more tickets. This, in turn, would require more time and effort, both of which are very precious commodities to Richard. Richard believes that to make a raffle effective, you need a desirable item to raffle, a reasonable ticket price, and sufficient time and help to sell enough tickets to meet your objectives.

## ■ ■ ■ It's Easier to Sell an Item than Oneself

Richard is among the majority of sponsored riders when he says that, "Asking for money is the most difficult aspect of fundraising." It is this aversion that made Richard experiment with different fundraising ideas.

Richard approached the husband of a boarder at his farm who works for Gore-Tex and inquired if Gore-Tex would be willing to enter into a sponsorship agreement with him. Although they were not amenable to making a cash contribution, they were willing to make a donation of material. Richard's friend then found a way to have the Gore-Tex fabric made up into hats promoting anything the customer desired. To date, Richard says that selling the hats has been the most successful fundraising venture for him. He feels it is much easier to go to someone with something to sell rather than just asking for money.

Richard is currently working with Outback Trading Company on a promotional deal. Gore-Tex's expectations of Richard are simple – he is only expected to return goodwill. Outback Trading will also expect a return in the form of goodwill, as well as product endorsement and Richard's name and picture in ads. In exchange, Richard hopes to receive some funding for his horse.

## ■ ■ ■ Raising Money Through Direct Mail

Richard has experimented with direct mail by sending letters to affluent people describing his plan and his needs. He did receive a few donations ranging from $10 to $200. Richard says that there are two important criteria that potential sponsors should meet before you go to the effort of sending direct mail requests:

- they must have an interest in horses, and

- they must be in a financial position where they can donate money.

After contacting prospective sponsors by mail, Richard calls them on the phone and arranges face-to-face visits whenever possible. Again, he says that he finds this to be much easier if he has something more to sell than just himself.

## ■ ■ ■ The Right Contacts Make All the Difference

In the whole scheme of things, Richard believes that it is who you know – either directly or indirectly – that is the most important factor in finding sponsorship. You either have to know the right people or know people who know the right people. Although Richard did not know Pat Goodman directly, he had a student who was willing and able to make the contact for him. The key is to inform enough people of your objectives so that word of your endeavors eventually falls upon the right ears.

Thanks to Richard's student's conversation with Pat Goodman, Richard and Cestus have been winning partners since 1992.

# Lisa Kulski Finds Sponsors Without Actively Looking

### ■ ■ ■ Profile

Since age 9, Lisa Kulski has been actively striving to improve her riding, training, and competition skills through continuous training with well-qualified instructors. She received her initial instruction through her involvement in Pony Club and since then has worked with numerous top dressage trainers.

In 1979, a seemingly minor event occurred that changed the course of Lisa's riding and her life. Although Lisa graduated from the University of Vermont with a degree in Clinical Microbiology, she soon found her career on an entirely different track. An avid event rider, Lisa boarded at an event barn in North Ferrisburg, Vermont. The owner of the farm and a boarder had scheduled a lesson with dressage trainer Jane Savoie, but at the last minute, the boarder had to cancel. Lisa opted to take her place and this single decision radically changed both her riding goals and her career goals.

Lisa gained experience as a working student for FEI level dressage rider/trainer Kathy Connelly before striking off on her own at the New England

Equestrian Center in Shelburne, Vermont in 1988. NEEC is an 18-acre, 30-stall facility with a large enough lesson load to support four full-time instructors and a staff of eight that manages the daily care of the horses. The farm has 20 boarders, approximately 10 school horses, and they give, on average, 50 lessons per week.

Over the years, Lisa has worked with Sue Shirland, Pam Goodrich, Gunnar Ostergaard, Bill Woods, and Major Andres Lindgren. She currently trains with Kevin Edwards on her three sponsored horses.

## ■ ■ ■ The Sponsors and Their Agendas

Although FEI rider Lisa Kulski is not yet a dressage household name the way Reiner Klimke or Anky Van Grunsven are, that was in no way detrimental to her being able to find sponsorship. In fact, Lisa enjoys the assistance provided by four sponsors who help her in various ways. All four are private sponsors and all sought out Lisa rather than her finding them. As Lisa says, "It may not have worked with some of my sponsors if I had actively been seeking sponsorship."

People provide sponsorship for various reasons, and Lisa's sponsors have their own unique reasons for supporting Lisa's efforts. Lisa's first sponsor was impressed by Lisa's dedication and focus, the second was interested in the performing arts, the third felt good about investing money in a top dressage rider, and the fourth invested for both business and personal reasons.

One of Lisa's sponsors is in public relations and guides Lisa's business activities. She advised Lisa to sell two-thirds of her farm thereby providing Lisa with some needed cash while relieving her of some of the stress associated with operating the facility. This same sponsor writes articles that promote the farm and keep Lisa in the public eye. This has strengthened Lisa's base of operations and substantially increased the farm's lesson load.

Each sponsor is involved for a different reason, with a different agreement, and a different amount of financial support. All sponsors have their horses insured for major medical and mortality. One sponsor has a written contract.

## ■ ■ ■ Name Recognition

When Lisa's first two sponsors arrived on the scene, her name recognition was local and regional. By the time sponsors three and four came along, she had gained some national recognition through her competition record in New England and Florida. Lisa says that with private sponsors, the degree to which name recognition matters depends on the sponsor. Two of her sponsors are not

Mary Phelps photo

*"Private sponsors are not publicity driven," explains FEI level dressage rider Lisa Kulski. "They want to be sure they are sponsoring something they can feel good about."*

concerned while the other two are concerned only from the standpoint of Lisa's career.

### ■ ■ ■ Coping with a Nearly Devastating Setback

Lisa explains that each sponsor has offered something unique and valuable; however, it has not been smooth sailing throughout. Lisa tells of a nearly devastating experience that she thought was the end of her career. One of her sponsors purchased a very promising horse for Lisa to train and compete. Not long after the purchase of this horse, what every horse person fears became Lisa's true life experience. Due to an unfortunate turn of fate, the horse colicked. The best efforts of Lisa and her veterinarian were not enough to save him. Lisa says, "I was hysterical thinking my life is over, my career is over. My sponsor won't ever want to do this again. It was absolutely the lowest of lows for me." The sponsorship was relatively new, and Lisa was not sure she had gained the rapport necessary to make an endeavor like this work.

Naturally, the owner/sponsor was disappointed to lose such a promising horse, but Lisa was fortunate in having a sponsor who understands the insidious nature of colic. The sponsor was not deterred by this unfortunate loss and her faith in Lisa was in no way compromised. When the insurance money came through, Lisa was given the opportunity to purchase another horse.

### ■ ■ ■ Honesty and Integrity

Private sponsorships, such as Lisa's, are not profit driven. Lisa's four sponsors are interested in the well-being of their horses, Lisa's progress as a rider and trainer, and the enjoyment derived from owning well-represented, top quality horses. Lisa is completely honest with her sponsors regarding the risk of investing in horses. "You always hope to be able to sell the horse for a profit," says Lisa, "but that should not be the goal when going into such a venture." She stresses the importance of honesty and integrity in everything – from what you tell your sponsors to your day-to-day behavior. This is a major factor in keeping sponsors involved.

It may surprise some people to learn that Lisa's greatest satisfaction is not having qualified for national championships at every level with each horse, instead, it is "the validation they [the sponsors] provide. I have these four people who are willing to back me heart, soul, and pocketbook. It means a lot to have sponsors watch me train." She goes on to say, "Private sponsors are not publicity driven. They want to be sure they are sponsoring something they can feel good about."

When asked how sponsorship has affected her career, Lisa, without hesitation, responds, "Without my sponsors I wouldn't be where I am now. I would still be struggling along."

# Richard Shrake's Dual Roles as Sponsored Rider and Sponsor

### ■■■ Profile

Richard Shrake began showing at age nine and by 18 he was the owner and operator of his own show barn. He started out competing at the open shows and was active in training riders for the AHSA western equitation finals. For over 20 years, Richard hauled 30 to 35 riders to each show.

When breed shows became popular, Richard chose the Quarter Horse. He has held his Quarter Horse judge's card for 20 years; during this time, he has judged the World Show twice, the Paint World Show three times, and the Appaloosa World Show three times. He has judged the Arabian National and World Show six times, as well as Pintos, English, Western, and conformation. He showed the high point horse for the Quarter Horse Congress in the Western division and one of his students showed the same horse in the English division. Out of 10,000 horses, they were awarded the high point horse award.

Richard has produced 40 World Champion riders, and four years in a row he was voted one of the most popular judges in the United States in a poll done by *Horses* magazine. With 15 horse training videos and two training books to his credit, Richard is working on a third book and, as proof of his versatility, recently finished designing nine bits for Miller Harness Company.

Richard trained with Jimmy Williams – who actually started out as a western trainer before gaining national acclaim as a hunter/jumper trainer. Richard would stay with Jimmy for weeks at a time and spend entire summers training with him. Currently, Richard spends six out of every eight weeks traveling for his business. The other two weeks, he is at home at Winning Way Ltd. with his wife, Lee Ann, in Sunriver, Oregon.

Lee Ann oversees the scheduling of Richard's clinics and demonstrations, informs his sponsors of his activities and whereabouts, administers their apprentice program, and is responsible for designing and marketing Richard's books and videos. Although not a horse person herself, Lee Ann's marketing, organizational, and communications skills are invaluable to Richard's business success. Through a phone interview with Lee Ann, I was able to gather the following information on Richard's sponsorship activities.

### ■ ■ ■ Finding Sponsors

When Richard was in his late 20s, he approached and secured a small, short term sponsorship agreement with Purina. Over time, Richard's sponsorships have grown and he now names his sponsors as Purina, Triple Crown Fences, and Triple Crown Feed.

Although Richard had a sponsorship with Purina more than 20 years ago, it had lapsed by the time he started making his training videos and needed some financial assistance. Fortunately, Purina's CEO Les Brewer, who Richard had worked with originally, was still with Purina and remembered Richard. "I don't know if it would have been as simple if Les hadn't still been there," says Lee Ann.

Purina and the Shrakes work with an ad agency to promote Richard's videos and Purina's feeds. Because of the mutually beneficial relationship between the Shrakes and Purina, the ad agency put together a similar sponsorship program for the Shrakes with Freedom Feeder and Triple Crown Fencing. "Triple Crown had been looking for someone and the ad agency put us together because of our association with Purina," says Lee Ann.

### ■ ■ ■ What Richard Provides to His Sponsors

"We help with the Purina Gold program – Purina Gold dealers are dealers who buy a large amount of Purina product" says Lee Ann. "When Richard is going

*Richard Shrake has been in the horse business since age 18 and not only has sponsors, but also sponsors some of his students.*

to be in a particular area, I let Purina know so that they can contact their Purina Gold dealers and arrange for Richard to do a program for them.

"Purina's programs are free to the public and are advertised in the paper and on the radio. They are always held at a large local facility and usually last for three to three and a half hours," explains Lee Ann. "It is an opportunity for Purina to introduce the Purina feed products and to break into a lot of different areas that they haven't been in to. They have a lot of new products that people are not yet aware of. Purina's District Manager begins the program by talking about Purina products and answering feed related questions. The manager makes sure that all of the attendees' questions are answered and then turns the floor over to the other invited speakers: farriers, veterinarians, trainers, and other equine professionals. When it is time for Richard's demonstration, he is given a halter-broken two-year-old that he will saddle and back in one and a half to two hours. He then answers training questions from the crowd. We have been doing a lot of these programs," says Lee Ann, "and we are currently doing the same thing for Triple Crown Fence and the Freedom Feeder.

"We have written agreements describing what we will do for our sponsors and what they are providing to us. To really do the sponsors justice, three is about all anybody can handle," says Lee Ann. "The contracts are renewable and are normally for one- to three-year periods. Lee Ann goes on to describe Richard's sponsorships as a "pyramid type of thing." Richard receives sponsorships from three companies and, in turn, provides sponsorship to some of his students.

## ■■■The Image Factor

"Image is important to corporations," explains Lee Ann. "Honesty, integrity with our business, and running everything in a businesslike manner is important to our sponsors. And, probably most of all, being a good steward with their name.

"Keeping the sponsors informed of what we are doing and keeping their name out there is important. We are working to increase their exposure and market share, and it is important to them to have their products represented in the right light. Every month, and sometimes more frequently, I send Richard's sponsors printouts telling them his plans, changes in plans, and an inventory of what we need in the way of literature or product for our booth."

### ■ ■ ■ Increasing and Benefiting by Name Recognition

Richard has been in the horse business for so many years, that when he called Miller Harness Company to ask if they would be interested in the bits he had designed, he had a ready buyer. "It is a little easier for Richard compared to a lot of people that are out there because pretty much everybody does know his name," says Lee Ann. "He is really out there working for the sponsors. We both are. He is promoting his sponsors' products.

"As far as Miller, they are not a sponsor per se," continues Lee Ann. "They are marketing a product for us and we work with them on a royalty basis. It is the same situation with the books Richard has written. Sponsorships give us more national recognition by Richard's appearing in their ads and at large expos.

"Sponsors help us with the cost of producing Richard's training videos," explains Lee Ann. "They help us financially and they help us with product. They also do national advertising for us. Triple Crown has Richard in about four or five national magazines, which is to our benefit, and I think Purina has two national ads coming up this year in the *Quarter Horse Journal* and *Western Horseman* magazine that feature Richard. Every year, as we work more and more closely together, we do more for them and they do more for us. And we just keep the relationship going and it gets stronger."

### ■ ■ ■ Gaining Exposure Through Horse Fairs

Horse fairs are big events that are usually put on by state horse councils. They are typically held on fairgrounds and people will come from several states away to attend. These fairs serve to bring horse people and non-horse people together. They introduce the different breeds and disciplines of riding so that people of varying levels of skill and interest can benefit by attending. "They have a parade of horses and a parade of breeds. Some are just a kick," says Lee Ann. "Richard did the Virginia Horse Festival in Lexington with 25,000 people. They featured Jack Russell Terrier races, which are really fun. Although the fair revolves around horses, it appeals to a lot of different people. People will come to watch the dog races and get involved in the horses.

"We were the first people to go into horse fairs. They used to only use local state talent until eight years ago when I almost had to get on my knees to get the horse fair in Illinois to bring in people from outside. That was the first horse fair we did," says Lee Ann. "Richard's presence there tripled their attendance, and the whole idea has snowballed since then with our participating in seven expos in 1996. Because Richard's picture appears frequently in horse magazines, many people recognize him and will attend expos where he is giving clinics and demonstrations. This helps us sell more videos and books. It builds on itself."

## ■■■ Giving Back to the Community

It's important to realize that one must be willing to give back to get something. And some people give back more than others. Such is the case with Richard Shrake, who is civic-minded and willing to reach out to help others.

Richard did a clinic for 2,000 4-H children on a Friday at The Ohio Horse Fair, which attracts about 80,000 attendees. "The Fair provides a lot of sponsoring to their state 4-H," says Lee Ann. "These were kids who would not have been able to attend such a clinic. They couldn't really afford to come to Richard for training. So these fairs open up doors that are otherwise closed to some kids."

Richard was the first trainer to work with the Bureau of Land Management's (BLM) wild horse program. He approached them out of concern for the abuse of wild horses and produced a video for them. "He actually went into the federal penitentiary program and worked with men who were in there for life by teaching them how to train wild horses," says Lee Ann. "He said it was an experience he'll never forget because it was like 'who was training whom?' You could see the change in the men as well as the horses. There was some turmoil because the prison's horse trainers resented his coming in and saying 'you don't have to be abusive and this is how you train these horses. You do it through patience, you do it through kindness, and you just be there for them. If they get upset, you don't get upset with them.' Some of these guys got upset because Richard's techniques differed from their own. But the point was, they couldn't fight the fact that it worked for the horses. It also worked for the inmates in their lives. We got letters from inmates afterwards. They came to us through the BLM and told Richard how much his training and their working with the horses had changed their lives. Most people don't know that Richard really got this thing started because once it was rolling, he went on to something else. The BLM did a tribute to Richard in Nevada in 1996."

## ■■■ The Pyramid

Along with promoting his sponsors' products, giving clinics and demos, producing videos, and writing books, Richard also sponsors some of his students.

Richard offers a three-part apprentice program designed for people who want a career with horses. His program is geared toward people who want to become finished riders, active competitors, and trainers of competition riders. He teaches showmanship, horsemanship, western pleasure, and western riding.

"We give scholarships for our graduate program," says Lee Ann. "We don't actually have a form for students to fill out. People who have gone through the first level of our training program, who have talent, and who want to be professional horse trainers but cannot afford the program are selected. We do that quite frequently now. It is hard to pick them up the first time around because we don't yet know if they are doing it just for the fun of it, and that is not what our program is for. It is for people who want to become instructors. A lot of companies that are laying people off have given them money to retrain for something else. So these people are using the money to go into the horse industry. Our program is qualified with U.S. West so that money obtained by laid-off workers for retraining can be used to go through our program.

"Our program consists of three sessions, and when students have completed our program, they are able to make money. We have instructors set up all over the U.S. If people cannot afford second and third sessions, we provide them with scholarships. Upon successful completion of the program, we assist our students by advertising them as *Resistance-Free Trainers*. We have created the business for them, and they have Richard behind them as well as the confidence to go out and get the customers. Our program provides them with a hotline. They can call in at any time to get Richard's number on the road and ask him questions on problematic situations they may encounter. They are required to attend one of Richard's clinics, at no charge, once a year. The goal is not to make big money from this end, but to get people out there using Richard's methods, which emphasize training without abuse, and to provide these people with a fulfilling career."

## ■ ■ ■ Name Recognition and Product Identity

Richard was well established in the horse industry when he found his sponsors. "Unless you are established, it is pretty hard to go out there and get sponsors," says Lee Ann. "Sponsors want people who are really going to be out there with the masses. Most trainers are so busy training horses, hauling horses, and going to shows that they aren't dealing with the public, and they certainly don't have time to promote a company's products. We've been there and done that [showing]. We would start in January in Florida and would haul 35 kids all over the U.S. year round. Richard spent 20 years doing that. When we started doing more clinics and putting out the videos and books, it allowed us, especially through the expos, to have access to thousands and thousands of people.

"When we set up our booth at an expo, we have a Purina banner and a

Triple Crown banner. We hand out their brochures, and we answer questions about their products. It is obvious to anyone visiting our booth who we represent. I make sure that whomever is working in the booth for us can answer questions. I always check with local dealers in the area to make sure that, if they are going to an expo that we are attending, they get a booth close to us so that they can reap some of the benefits of what we are doing."

Richard does not compete anymore, but he continues to teach, do clinics, write books, and produce videos. He has also designed a series of saddles for Circle Y called the Richard Shrake Resistance Free Saddle.

## ■ ■ ■ Advice on Finding a Sponsor

"Go to someone who already has a sponsor," recommends Lee Ann. "Ask what you should do." If you are trying to promote a product whether it be bits, videos, books, or whatever, she suggests asking someone with name recognition to test the product to see if it is something they would endorse. "Most everyone is going to have to start at the bottom," she says. "You have to pay your dues."

# The Sponsors

# Know Thy Sponsor

## ■ ■ ■ The Corporate Sponsor

It is imperative that you learn as much as you can about your potential sponsor's business and products. Just as you want to position yourself properly in order to obtain a sponsor, corporate sponsors want to position their products in such a way as to obtain the greatest market share possible.

Corporate sponsors choose riders who can ride well, present themselves well, and market their products effectively. By taking the initiative to learn about your potential sponsor's products, you demonstrate that you are interested in promoting their business rather than just benefiting by their largesse. As noted earlier, corporations provide sponsorship for all or some of the following reasons:

- to increase their sales

- to increase their visibility

- to educate customers on their products

- to differentiate their products from the competition

- to showcase their products in an upscale market

Information that will be helpful to you before approaching a corporate sponsor includes:

- learning about their product line

- learning who their competition is

- learning who their customers are (children, adults, sports enthusiasts, gardeners, etc.)

- learning how they market their products (i.e., TV, newspaper, radio ads, direct mail, telemarketing, etc.)

- getting background information on the company (when it was founded, number of employees, headquarters, etc.)

- getting the name, address, and direct number of the marketing director.

Much of this information can be obtained by contacting the company and requesting a copy of their annual report. You can usually get the name, address, and direct number of the marketing director from the company's receptionist. You can also request that product literature be sent to you. Public libraries are also a good source of information on larger companies.

You want to impress your potential sponsor by being familiar with their products and their history. This demonstrates your commitment and willingness to learn about and promote their company and product.

## ■ ■ ■ The Private Sponsor

Private sponsors' goals are different from those of corporate sponsors. And some of the information you will need is different, too.

You need to determine why the private sponsor is sponsoring you. It may be because of:

- their love of horses

- their personal interest in you

- the resale potential of the horse

- the prestige of owning a competition horse

- the enjoyment of traveling to competitions to watch their horse

- the desire to contribute to something they feel good about

These are only some of the reasons that an individual might sponsor you. Once you have determined what motivates your sponsor, you can modify your plan, if need be, to accommodate their goals.

## ■ ■ ■ Never Assume Anything

It is your responsibility to find out specifically what your sponsor is offering you. As uncomfortable as it may be to directly broach the subject of who pays for what, a thorough discussion on this topic is a must. Handling financial issues and clarifying each person's responsibilities will help you avoid aggravation, and possibly legal problems, at a later date. Although many of the riders interviewed did not have written contracts with their sponsors, most of them did have a clear understanding of who was providing what.

There is no foolproof method for a perfect sponsorship relationship; however, the more information you have at the beginning, the less likely it will be that you have a problem later.

# The Right Demographics Influence Corporate Sponsors

Providing your potential corporate sponsor with demographics on spectators and competitors at horse shows is of enormous value to them and to you. By demonstrating the popularity of horse sports, your chances of finding a corporate sponsor increase.

The following information was provided by the organizers of the Hampton Classic Horse Show – Executive Director Anthony Hitchcock, co-Executive Director Jean Lindgren, and Director of Media Relations Diana De Rosa.

### ■ ■ ■ Research Shows that Horse Show Spectators and Exhibitors are the Most Demographically Upscale of Any Sports Audience

Research material compiled for the Hampton Classic Horse Show (the country's largest hunter/jumper competition) indicates that the spectator/participant at a horse show is a member of a very influential group. Because of their education, income, profession and age – and more importantly, their interest in horses and horse shows – they are a group to be reckoned with by those corporations seeking an upscale market, as well as those wanting to reach a broader marketing spectrum.

## Statistics Overview

| | | |
|---|---|---|
| Age | 80% | 18-49 years of age |
| Income | 40% | $150,000+ family income |
| Education | 80% | College educated |
| Occupation | 35% | Business executives |
| Residence | 45.3% | Semi-rural |
| Home value | Average | $421,000 |
| 1+ homes | 27.2% | |

## Marketing Overview

| | | |
|---|---|---|
| Airline travel | 43.1% | 16+ trips per year . |
| Travel frequency | 78.4% | Member Frequent Flyer Club |
| Credit cards | 97.3% | One or more cards |
| Automobiles | 55.3% | Bought an auto w/in last 12 months |

This is an active and highly influential group with significant purchasing power. The demographic profile indicates that they have a high degree of education and strong opinions on product quality, value, and performance. This is a group which is a natural target-market for sponsors offering first-quality products and/or services.

Again, this is the most upscale demographic profile represented by any sport, representing an occupational mix, and linked by their interest in horses and competitive English riding.

## ■ ■ ■ Getting the Information Your Sponsor Needs

The right demographics are absolutely essential to your sponsor. The section above provides some important information and numbers. You now need to take the next step and contact the organizers of the big competitions you intend to compete in to request copies of any demographic information that they have available.

Obviously, smaller competitions may not have this information. Competitions such as the *Hampton Classic* have extensive information available to potential sponsors and other interested parties. Information about the 1996 Hampton Classic that would be of interest to potential sponsors includes the following:

Expected attendance        60,000-70,000

Number of horses expected   1,400

Prize money                $375,000

Audience

> CEOs from large corporations, writers, artists, entertainers, guests from television, the music industry, the fashion world, and Hollywood

Magazine/newspaper coverage

> *Harper's Bazaar, Town & Country, New York Magazine, Newsday, People, The New York Times, Vogue, W, Women's Wear Daily*

Television coverage

> The $100,000 Hampton Classic Grand Prix is telecast nationally to approximately 40,000,000 homes domestically plus additional homes in Canada, Central America, and South America. In all, the Hampton Classic is telecast to more than 200,000,000 households in over 100 countries through its coverage by Gillette World of Sports.

Benefits

> The Hampton Classic is a 501(c)3 charitable corporation and benefits Southampton Hospital's East End H.I.V./AIDS Center, the Nassau/Suffolk Chapter of the Juvenile Diabetes Foundation, and the United States Equestrian Team.

Program from previous year

> The program includes the prize list and advertising. Potential sponsors can review the list of past sponsors and advertisers to determine if this is a show that would be suitable for them to be affiliated with.

### ■ ■ ■ Corporate Sponsorship Amenities

Large competitions offer a number of venues for their corporate sponsors: full-page color advertising in their program, banners displayed over grandstands, public address announcements, participation in awards ceremonies by company representatives, local or national television commercial units, and more.

Corporations can sponsor classes – for instance, the Grand Prix – by providing the prize money. Typical corporate sponsorships at a competition such as the Hampton Classic range in price from approximately $10,000 to $100,000. Most show organizers will design individual packages to meet the needs of a particular corporate sponsor.

It is easy to see why demographics are of value to sponsors. Don't be timid about contacting competition organizers; they want their show to be a success and will be happy to provide you with demographic information that could bring them another sponsor.

# Miller Harness Company Backs Riders with Staying Power

Miller Harness Company has a long list of sponsored riders including Jumper riders Debbie Shaffner Stephens, Susie Hutchison, Anne Kursinski, Michael Matz, Margie Goldstein-Engle, Chris Kappler, and Hugh and Bert Mutch; dressage riders Dr. Reiner Klimke, Robert Dover, and Charlotte Bredahl; three-day eventer Bruce Davidson; World champion endurance rider Valerie Kanavy; Quarter Horse champion Lynn Salvatori Palm; and Canadian jumper riders Jill Henselwood and Mac Cone.

Beside their winning ways, these riders all share at least one other important trait – they have been successful over a period of time on a number of different horses. None of them rose to fame on one or two great horses and then disappeared from sight when those horses' careers were over. Rather, they continue to be leaders in their respective disciplines in national and international competitions.

### ■ ■ ■ Miller's Objectives and Expectations

Gaining product credibility and remaining prominently in the public eye are two of Miller's biggest objectives in sponsoring riders. By sponsoring top riders, Miller receives publicity opportunities beyond their catalogs and advertisements, and their products are given credibility by the fact that well-known riders are using them. As John Craven, International Wholesaler and Sponsorship Specialist for Miller Harness Company says, "Riding is too risky to use inferior equipment. They [the top riders] are not going to use something that doesn't work."

Part of the riders' contract with Miller is that they agree to make appearances at shows where a Miller dealer has a booth. They talk with customers and frequently sign autographs. "Sponsored riders attend our trade shows and discuss the product line with customers," explains John. "By their meeting the public and answering questions, they are providing a valuable educational service to the equine community. People ask training questions, product-related questions, and advice on what equipment to use."

### ■ ■ ■ Benefits to the Sponsoree

"All of our sponsored riders get a package from us at least once a year. It includes saddle pads with Miller's name embroidered on both sides, visors and baseball caps with Miller printed on them, anti-sweat sheets, coolers, and a variety of other products – all embroidered with Miller's name," says John. "They also receive a retail account with a credit that they can draw from to purchase what they want."

### ■ ■ ■ Media Coverage of Equestrian Sports

"As sponsors, lack of TV coverage is a concern for us. Many people have tried to address this issue over the years," says John. "There is significant coverage in European countries because riding in Europe has a longer history than in the U.S. and wider public appeal. We are just starting to see horse sports on cable networks, but there is a long way to go."

John believes that the lack of good commentators is a big part of the problem. "Even non-horse people find watching jumpers on TV enjoyable as long as there is a good commentator. I think there is an analogy to be made between figure skating and equestrian sports – not long ago figure skating was in the background until someone took an interest and did a good job commentating. Now figure skaters are household names. Ideally, a similar thing will happen in the horse industry," says John optimistically.

# Beval, Ltd. Sponsors Events and Individuals

### ■ ■ ■ Background

Beval, Ltd. is a family owned and operated tack shop specializing in English riding equipment. It was founded by Mark Walter's father in 1955, and was originally located in Bernardsville, New Jersey. The business is currently run by Mark, his mother and sister, and one partner.

Beval's hub is a 13,000 sq.ft. building in Gladstone, New Jersey, where they are involved in importing, wholesaling, and retailing. Their retail sites include a shop in New Canaan, Connecticut and a mobile unit that travels to most of the major hunter/jumper competitions.

Mark showed in equitation, Medal/Maclay, and hunter/jumpers until about 15 years ago. He was competing and taking Beval's mobile unit to shows, but found that the business activity became too time-consuming for him to continue competing. Mark now enjoys ownership of one horse for recreation and devotes most of his energy to running Beval.

Beval is a true saddler and warrants all of their products. Repairs can be done by Beval so that equipment does not have to be shipped back to the manufacturer. Beval imports the Butet saddle from France, which is currently one of the most desirable jumping saddles available.

### ■ ■ ■ Jumper Rider Beezie Patton as Beval's Spokesperson

Mark became acquainted with Beezie Patton about 15 years ago when she visited Beval's mobile unit. Through the mobile unit, Mark has come to know most of the Grand Prix riders on a first name basis. "The mobile unit is a good thing for us because we are always right there at the pulse of the industry," says Mark.

"We are entering into our fifth year of sponsoring Beezie," continues Mark, "She was the first person we sponsored. I approached Beezie at the Washington International Horse Show because I thought the exposure would be good for the company. I thought that Beezie would be the right person to represent us because of the quality of her riding and her tactfulness. We're not super flash – we're just down the middle, there all the time. A real saddlery. I felt that she fit into our program and would accurately project Beval's image."

Other riders sponsored by Beval include Peter Leone, Laura Chapot, and McLain Ward.

### ■ ■ ■ Impact of Sponsorships on Business

"Unfortunately, the value of sponsorship is a hard thing to put your finger on," says Mark. "What we hope to get out of it is to have our sponsored riders talk to people in the business and point them in our direction. Also, the fact that our name is out there in the Grand Prix ring is beneficial. Especially now that there is some TV coverage in the sport. But it's hard to put a real number [in terms of sales] on sponsorship. I do feel that it is a good thing for us.

"We are now sponsoring five riders. We supply them with equipment that we are considering adding to our product line. They test the equipment and give us their opinions. This is beneficial to us because it gives us the opportunity to improve our product."

### ■ ■ ■ Benefits To and Expectations of the Sponsoree

Beezie has saddle pads, coolers, and anti-sweat sheets with Beval's name on them. Using the sponsor's products at public events is one of the requirements of sponsorship. Beezie is on the cover of the 1996 catalog, and she has Beval trunks in her tack stall at shows as well as a display of Beval saddle pads. "Our mobile unit is usually at the same shows as Beezie," says Mark, "and in it we

Gary J. Benson photo

*Beval Ltd. sponsors several jumper riders including Beezie Patton shown above clearing the Beval jump.*

have catalogs available to customers. Beezie is occasionally called upon to distribute catalogs as well.

"We issue our riders an annual credit amount for equipment for them or their staff. In addition, if they win a Grand Prix of over $25,000, they are given an additional credit. A few years ago, Beezie won quite a few Grand Prix classes so her credit just kept going up and up. The more the riders win, the more they get [from Beval]. Plus they get all the horse clothes. And if we have any logo wear (for example, hats, shirts, or jackets), they are supplied with all of that."

## ■ ■ ■ Beval Sponsors Competitions As Well As Individuals

"We have an agreement with Stadium Jumping, Inc., who arranges major jumper shows throughout the country. They arrange for a space for our mobile unit on the horse show grounds and for the display of two of our banners in the show ring," explains Mark. "Additionally, there is a jump with our name painted on it. This is all included in the sponsorship package they offer. What we sponsor is a lot of the equitation classes rather than the big Grand Prix classes like Crown Royal. The Grand Prix are a more expensive way to go. Saddlery-wise we are one of the longest standing sponsors."

# Natasha Grigg Enjoys Sponsoring a Friend

### ■ ■ ■ Profile

Natasha Grigg resides in Boxford, Massachusetts with her husband and six horses and ponies. She is an active driving judge and competes her own Welsh ponies at major East coast competitions. Natasha describes herself as "horse crazy since childhood." While living in Colorado as a child, Natasha was taught to ride by her father. Although her riding was interrupted by her family's move to a metropolitan area, she never lost interest in horses.

Because of her Russian parentage, Natasha has spoken Russian all of her life and majored in Russian literature in college and graduate school. While in college, she secured a high paying job as an interpreter during the cultural exchange between the Soviet Union and the U.S., thus enabling her to purchase a horse. She stabled her mare at the Claremont Riding Academy in New York City until graduation, when her work schedule began to demand that she spend a great deal of time traveling with various dance companies, thus forcing her to give up her horse.

In 1966, Natasha married and moved to Massachusetts where she raised two "horse crazy daughters." In the early 70s, she bought a bay mare that resembled the horse she had had as a young woman and a companion pony. Natasha taught both herself and the 11 hand, Welsh-Hackney pony to drive, which was the beginning of her passion for driving. Welsh ponies were subsequently purchased from a neighbor who was teaching Natasha's two daughters to ride. When the children weren't available to ride the ponies, Natasha kept them fit by driving them. The snowball effect was in motion, and Natasha began breeding Welsh ponies. She also competed at the advanced level in the Singles division with her daughter's Fourth level dressage horse. "He was fabulous. When he was 13 years old I trained him to drive," says Natasha. "I don't claim any credit for him. He was just a great horse. He is 25 years old, and I still have him."

Natasha's compassion, deep respect, and love for her animals is borne out by the fact that they are not discarded when she can no longer use them. They are either retired to a life of comfort and good care at her Boxford farm, or, as in the case of two of her Trakehners, they are on loan to a local therapeutic riding program.

Natasha is currently competing her homebred Palomino Welsh Cob pair and training a pair of homebred Welsh Arabs. She still finds the time to do a lot of judging for the American Driving Society.

## ■■■ Helping Others

Rather than just being sympathetic to the plight of talented horse people with limited funds, Natasha Grigg has actively gone out and done something about it. An avid driver, judge, and competitor, Natasha has helped several individual riders and has been a force behind the success of driver and dressage rider Larry Poulin.

Natasha and Larry became acquainted in the mid-70s. Larry was working for Margaret Gardiner, owner of Kennebec Morgan Horse Farm in Wiscasset, Maine, driving Margaret's herd stallion, Kennebec Count. He went on to drive Kennebec Count and his son Kennebec Russell as a pair. Natasha says, "There was no stopping Larry. He won four USET pair championships with that pair and represented the U.S. abroad." As the Morgan pair got older, Larry needed a new opportunity.

## ■■■ The Implicit Difficulties of Driving Sponsorships

"Finding sponsorship for driving is a little more complicated than other types of sponsorships," explains Natasha. "Most of the supporters of driving are

Ronni Nienstedt photo

*"This venture has just between Larry and myself," says sponsor Natasha Grigg (seated in carriage with Larry Poulin). "I sponsored Larry because I wanted him to have this opportunity and not have to worry about anyone taking it away again."*

drivers themselves. What frequently happens is that a driver will find a sponsor, but then the sponsor wants to drive the horses himself, so that takes care of that. Larry has never had sufficient financial resources, or the right horses to be completely independent as an international caliber competitor. He has always been dependent on other people to make it possible for him to compete nationally and internationally. Many talented people don't have the money."

## ■ ■ ■ The Fan Club

Larry was fortunate to have the support of several sponsors prior to Natasha. First, there was the aforementioned Margaret Gardiner, who provided the Morgan stallions with whom he competed in Germany at the World Pair Championship, as well as all over the United States, winning the USET Pair Championship with them a number of times. Another sponsor, Mr. Kohler, owned the Warmbloods that Larry drove in the Hungarian World Pair Championship for the USET. When that sponsorship ended, Natasha and a group of Larry's friends (which Natasha refers to as his 'fan club') arranged for him to have horses and carriages in order to compete as an individual in the 1993 World Pair Championship at Gladstone, New Jersey. Pair owner/competitor Joseph Jayson loaned Larry his Cleveland Bay mares and the fan club helped finance the venture. "They contributed money to help feed, stable, and transport these animals so that Larry could fulfill the requirements of competing in a certain number of selection trials," explains Natasha.

## ■ ■ ■ Natasha Grigg Steps In as Sole Sponsor

All of Larry's sponsorships until 1994 had been short-term solutions, and in 1994 he was again without a pair of driving horses. While Natasha was competing her pony pair in Gladstone, she was stabled next to Spencer Kipe and his three Hungarian driving horses. Spencer had purchased these horses from Hungarian driving champion Lazlo Kesckemeti several years earlier. "Spencer is an amateur driver and a very nice man," says Natasha. "I met him when we were competing single horses together. He told me that he wasn't having a good time and wasn't doing well with this pair. I spoke to his groom and during the weekend I was sort of checking them [Spencer's horses] out. Although they were older horses – 16, 13, and 11 – I really liked them; I liked what I saw, and I liked their attitude. They are not supremely fancy nor are they that young, but they are *good* horses. So I asked Spencer if he would consider loaning them to Larry, and he said yes. I then talked Larry into accepting the loan."

Since Larry was without a marathon carriage, Natasha was able to provide him with one. Larry drove these horses for the first time at Fair Hill in October 1994. He arrived at the competition just three days in advance and went on to win it. Natasha later bought the three horses and turned them over to Larry.

When asked why she elected to sponsor Larry, Natasha answers, "I don't know why the bug bit me. It was just spontaneous. There I was in Gladstone at a major competition, there were lots of pairs competing, and there was this guy [Larry] who I knew should have been there beating them all, but he wasn't, because he did not have the financial wherewithal. And there was this owner who was not getting the satisfaction he had hoped for from his horses.

"This venture has been a venture just between Larry and myself," continues Natasha. "I sponsored Larry because I wanted him to have this opportunity without having to worry about it being taken away again. He is a born horseman, half horse, a natural. He understands horses and is amazing with them. He is beautiful to watch."

## ■■■ Poulin's Winning Attributes

"Larry is always very experimental," says Natasha. "In pair driving, each competitor has three horses: 'the pair and a spare.' These horses must be declared before the beginning of the competition. The driver begins the competition with two horses and may only make one change of horses throughout the competition. Larry would switch horses and do various combinations to see who worked well in which phase of the competition. It takes a very long time to find these things out and to develop a partnership. So he took these risks while he was also trying out for the Team. Most people wouldn't take chances like that because they are afraid. But he did take chances and represented the U.S. in Poznan, Poland in August 1995 along with Lisa Singer and Vance Courthauld. Lisa and Vance are also sponsored drivers. Lisa drives Mimi Thorrington's Morgans, and Vance drives for Jack Wetzel.

"To finish the triumphant story, In the fall of 1995, exactly a year after I had seen these horses, Larry won the USET Pair Championship with them. That was glorious. A great finish to a wonderful year."

## ■■■ Independence Gained Through a Sponsor

"Larry now has his own horses and equipment and is no longer beholden to various patrons and sponsors, which is basically how I wanted to do it," says Natasha. "I did it for myself and for him. Driving is fundamentally a rich man's sport. There are many instances where someone else will do all the training and the owner hops in five minutes before the competition. I really don't like that. And I don't like to see horses treated as a commodity. I got tired over the years of watching Larry spend all this energy and time and then have the horses taken away. It happens regularly and in other disciplines as well. There are many agreements where a syndicate acquires a horse for you, you take it to the highest levels, and then they sell it for a great deal of money. It is wonderful that there are interested and generous people who wish to donate horses either to the USET or individual competitors, but I think a lot of sponsors do it without being aware of what it means when the partnership is dissolved. That is not going to happen to Larry. He has a new horse – a young Latvian horse. This horse will probably replace one of the older horses who will go into retirement."

When asked about past or future sponsorships, Natasha replies, "I have helped some friends of mine who ride by giving some money here and there. And I hope to continue to do so. Larry is launched now. I'll always be a friend and chip in if necessary, but I think he has everything he needs; horses, carriages, harnesses, etc. I helped him get harnesses as well as a large trailer of his own, so now he is all set."

## ■ ■ ■ No Formal Agreement Between Friends

Larry and Natasha have never had any formal agreements. They are both from New England; friends for over 20 years with a shared interest. "I have watched him develop as a driver. I was not always his greatest admirer, but it was wonderful to watch him progress and become more refined as a driver. I think he is truly gifted, and I also like the underdog. I consider Larry to be the best pair driver in the country. He has become a very respected judge and is one of the favorite driving teachers in the country."

Thanks to Natasha's generous support, Larry is well on his way. He is based in Falmouth, Maine at his Highland Dressage Center where he teaches ridden dressage and driving. As well as being a successful driver, he is also a respected driving judge and trainer, and he travels all over the country judging and giving driving clinics.

# A Message From the Sponsors

### ■ ■ ■ Tracking Sponsorship Results

State Line Tack in Plaistow, New Hampshire has been sponsoring riders since 1991. According to Promotions Manager Haley Blacklow, "Sports marketing results are very difficult to track. These efforts are very image-driven and need to be extremely specific and targeted if you hope to measure increases in sales generated through sponsorships." Nonetheless, State Line Tack and numerous other companies feel that there are benefits to offering sponsorships and they continue with their sponsorship programs for this reason.

### ■ ■ ■ Traits that Influence Sponsors

In a nutshell, traits of the sponsoree that are important to corporate sponsors are:

- equestrian skill
- outgoing personality

- articulateness
- willingness and ability to discuss the sponsor's products
- name recognition
- knowledge of the sponsor's products
- energy and enthusiasm
- willingness to work with the sponsor
- integrity
- honesty

Along with riding skill, personality is the most important factor to companies selecting sponsorees. Haley Blacklow succinctly sums up the prevailing attitude among corporate sponsors by saying, "They [the riders] don't have to be winning all the time. It's more important that they be well-respected in the industry and willing to work with us. Unlike a lot of sports, age does not matter."

## ■ ■ ■ Different Approaches to Achieve Different Goals

John Hamilton of the Dymar Agency (an ad agency that specializes in representing horse farms and equine products) worked with Purina to set up a sponsorship with Grand Prix dressage rider Betsy Steiner. As John says, "Purina selected Betsy because they were looking for a good spokesperson in the dressage world; someone who would be willing to educate people about equine nutrition. Betsy does numerous riding clinics all over the country and is willing to take time to discuss nutritional issues with participants."

In the past, Purina has sponsored high profile competitors. However, they have shifted their focus and are now taking more of a grassroots approach because they feel that they can reach a greater number of people that way.

In the final analysis, outgoing personality, articulateness, integrity, and willingness to work on the sponsor's behalf weighed in as the most important traits when corporate sponsors were selecting sponsorees. For private sponsors, personality, honesty and integrity, skill, and making the experience fun for the sponsor are the most important factors.

# The Value of Event Sponsorship

### ■ ■ ■ Dodge Truck Rodeo

In 1981, Dodge Truck Rodeo was founded for the purpose of promoting Dodge trucks through the sport of rodeo. Dodge Truck Rodeo president Jack Lowry and a staff of 19 attend to all of the logistical details surrounding the sponsorship of rodeo events. With over 300 events per year to oversee, each of the eight regional managers log 50,000 to 100,000 miles per year on their trucks as they travel around the country meeting with Dodge truck dealers. It is their job to get local dealers involved in sponsoring rodeos and to offer any support the dealers might need so that they derive the maximum benefit from sponsoring the event.

### ■ ■ ■ Awards and Challenges

Dodge offers awards programs through the Professional Rodeo Cowboys Association (PRCA) including the Dodge Truck Series, which is a program where Dodge keeps track of the winners of the seven rodeo events: bull riding, saddle bronc riding, calf roping, team roping, steer wrestling, bareback riding, and girls barrel racing. At year end, the highest point winner in each category receives the use of a new Dodge truck for one year.

The Dodge Truck Bull Challenge is a cash prize awarded to the bull rider who successfully rides a particularly difficult bull. "We select 15 bulls from across the country to participate in our bull challenge program," says Jack. "They have to be very difficult to ride to be included in our program. Each time a particular bull is not successfully ridden, another $500 is added to the prize money. Currently we have two bulls who are at $12,000 and two that are at $13,000. In 1995, 18-year-old Corey Check took home $28,500 for riding Dodge Laramie II for eight seconds!

"The animals' well-being is very important to us and to the stock contractor," says Jack. "Any animal that is not 100% is put on an injured reserve list and a substitute bull will buck in his place, much like athletes in the other pro sports. For instance, one bull recently had his hooves trimmed a bit too short, which made him sore. He ended up on the injured reserve list. It wasn't serious, but this type of care ensures that the animal is given adequate time and treatment to fully recover."

## ■ ■ ■ Tracking Results

Dodge Truck Rodeo performs sophisticated statistical analyses to gain demographic data on the people who attend rodeo events.

At each of the 300 Dodge-sponsored rodeo events, Dodge has a sweepstakes drawing. Entrants fill out a questionnaire either at the rodeo or at a local Dodge dealer that is participating in the sweepstakes program. Information that they are asked to provide includes age, gender, income, home owner status, type of truck or car owned, when the entrant will be purchasing a new truck, what type of truck the entrant plans to purchase, etc. A drawing is held at each rodeo, and the winner receives a specially crafted belt buckle. That person is then entered in the grand prize sweepstakes, which is held at the National Rodeo Finals in December. The winner of the final drawing receives *The Ultimate Cowboy Rig* – a $75,000 package that includes a new Dodge Ram truck equipped with a Lance Squire camper, a Ramsey electric winch, and a three-horse Featherlite horse trailer with dressing room. With over half a million people entering these sweepstakes, Dodge Truck Rodeo is able to gather a prodigious amount of demographic data.

In addition to numerous local rodeos, Dodge sponsors the Dodge National Circuit Finals Rodeo (PRCA's second-most prestigious rodeo), and they co-sponsor the Wrangler World of Rodeo, which is broadcast on ESPN. Dodge is also the title sponsor of TNN's weekly broadcast of rodeo events.

### ■ ■ ■ Rodeo Facts that Influence Sponsors

- Rodeo is the third most popular sport in terms of ticket sales.

- In 1995 more than 46,000,000 people bought a professional rodeo ticket.

- The only sports that boast more live spectator participation than rodeo are auto racing and horse racing.

- Rodeo prize money in 1995 exceeded $24,000,000.

### ■ ■ ■ The Significance of Demographics

Collecting data on the attendees of sporting events and properly analyzing that data is critical to the success of sponsoring organizations. Because 500,000 people watch a particular event does not mean that that event is right for *any* sponsor. The audience has to be right for the particular product. For instance, a TV audience that is primarily made up of children between the ages of four and six is not going to be the right audience for the manufacturer of exotic cars. Obviously, their advertising dollars would be better spent elsewhere. As Jack Lowry says regarding event sponsorship, "It is a matter of carefully targeting your market so that you know who your customers are."

This is why it is important for sponsorees to understand the demographics of their particular discipline. You can save a lot of time by learning what type of audience your sport appeals to and then determining what companies would benefit by making themselves visible in that particular market.

# Rodeo Events Appeal
# to Corporate Sponsors

R odeo has proven to be the equestrian sport of first choice for corporate sponsors because of the audience it reaches and the TV coverage it receives.

It is through the dedication and hard work of the staff of the Professional Rodeo Cowboys Association (PRCA) that rodeo events receive excellent media coverage. PRCA is located in Colorado Springs, Colorado and is the largest rodeo-sanctioning body in the world. In 1995, PRCA had more than 11,000 members and sanctioned rodeos that awarded in excess of $25.4 million in prize money. The National Finals Rodeo, which is held in Las Vegas each December, awarded over $3 million in prize money in 1995.

Some of the reasons PRCA has been so successful in securing large corporate sponsors include these facts:

- They have made significant efforts to gather and provide valuable demographic information to their prospective sponsors.
- They publicize their events extensively.

- Since 1991, PRCA has had an agreement with ESPN to broadcast nine rodeo events per year called "The Wrangler World of Rodeo."
- They offer specific programs to their sponsors.

## ■ ■ ■ Demographics of Rodeo Spectators and Competitors

The following survey information was gathered by PRCA.

- More than 85% of rodeo spectators own their homes and have spent an average of nearly 15 years at their current residence.

- Women and men enjoy professional rodeo in almost equal numbers. 51% of the spectators who answered the survey were women and 49% were men.

- Spectators fly an average of more than 3.7 times per year.

- Rodeo fans attend an average of 17 rodeos per year. Approximately 68% regularly follow rodeo standings and news.

- 31.9% have high school diplomas, 32.9% have attended college, 15% have college degrees, and 8.2% completed graduate school.

- 23.3% earn $35,000-49,999, 24.4% earn $50,000-74,999, and 17.6% earn over $75,000.

- 29.9% are Professionals, 15.4% are involved in Agriculture, 13.6% are Homemakers, 12.3% are involved in Technical/Trade, 9.2% are Secretaries/Clerks, 6.8% are involved in sales, and 12.8% are Other.

- 18.8% are 29 years old and under, 21.3% are 30-39, 25.7% are 40-49, and 34.2% are 50 and over.

These statistics are of tremendous value to corporate sponsors in helping them determine if the rodeo audience is the right market for their product or service. For companies whose products would appeal to PRCA's target audience, this information is valuable in helping them plan their marketing strategies.

## ■ ■ ■ Brand Loyalty of Rodeo Fans Motivates Sponsors

Another strong motivator for corporate sponsors of rodeo events is the brand loyalty demonstrated by PRCA fans. A study done for the PRCA indicates that rodeo fans and competitors are "fiercely loyal" to PRCA's sponsors' products.

- Approximately 93.6% of rodeo fans wear Western clothing at some time, while 61.2% wear it regularly.

- More than 19% of the survey respondents had purchased a Western hat within 60 days of the poll.

- Nearly 35% of those questioned had purchased cowboy boots during the previous 60 days.

- Some 18.5% had purchased a new belt buckle within 60 days of the poll.

- Tobacco products were purchased by 32.2% during the previous month. That compares with a national tobacco use average of 30%, according to the Tobacco Institute in Washington, DC.

- About 52.5% had purchased beer in the month prior to answering the questionnaire. Nationally, about 43% of the U.S. adult population consumes beer, according to the Beer Institute, headquartered in Washington, DC.

- More than 27% had purchased distilled spirits within a month of the survey.

- Soft-drink purchases by the respondents in the 30 days prior to the survey totaled 93.3%.

- Nearly 27% of those surveyed said they intend to buy a new car or light truck within a year.

It is not surprising that companies such as Wrangler jeans and shirts, Resistol hats, Copenhagen Skoal tobacco, Dodge Truck, and many others find it beneficial to sponsor rodeos. The rodeo audience is an ideal market for their products.

### ■ ■ ■ Rodeo Receives Excellent Television Coverage

Since 1991, ESPN has been running "The Wrangler World of Rodeo," which is a series of nine major rodeo events held each year. Because of the impressive viewership statistics, ESPN extended "The Wrangler World of Rodeo" contract by three years in 1993.

The nine televised rodeos are viewed by more than 17 million people, and the final performance of the National Finals Rodeo reaches more than five million viewers. Rodeo events prominently display sponsors' banners on the competition arena's walls, and many of these sponsors also buy TV advertising spots during these events.

## ■ ■ ■ Sponsorship Programs Available Through PRCA

PRCA has designed three programs to meet the specific needs of companies sponsoring their rodeo events. These programs are:

**Exclusive Sponsor** – This agreement ensures that no commercial enterprise selling products or services in competition with exclusive sponsors will be allowed to sponsor PRCA-sanctioned rodeos, nor will any such competitor's signage be displayed in the rodeo arena. The PRCA has exclusive sponsorship agreements with Copenhagen Skoal Pro Rodeo[SM] and Wrangler Jeans and shirts.

**First-Right-of-Refusal Sponsor** – First-right-of-refusal sponsors are given the opportunity to sponsor an event under the same terms and conditions offered by a competing commercial enterprise. If the first-right-of-refusal sponsor declines to participate, a competitor may sponsor the event. Coors Brewing Company and Dodge Truck are first-right-of-refusal sponsors.

**First-Consideration Sponsor** – The PRCA encourages rodeo producers to offer sponsorship rights to first-consideration sponsors before approaching competing sponsors; however, the rodeo committee/producer is not required to use first-consideration sponsors or to offer them sponsorship rights on the same terms and conditions offered to competitors. First-consideration sponsorship agreements exist between the PRCA and Coca-Cola USA, the House of Seagram (Crown Royal), Justin Boots, and Resistol hats.

More detailed information on the PRCA and its activities may be obtained by contacting:

The Professional Rodeo Cowboys Association
101 Pro Rodeo Drive
Colorado Springs, CO 80919

# Sports Agents, Insurance, Rules & Restrictions

# Using an Agency to Secure Sponsorship

Using an agency to secure sponsorship is a good route for established equestrians who have already achieved some level of name recognition. Agents have numerous contacts and can help connect you with a prospective sponsor, as well as help with your presentation. As Grand Prix jumper rider Mark Leone says, "They know the right people to call and the right doors to knock on."

"Sports agencies are in the business of negotiating contracts between corporations and athletes, and arranging public appearances and speaking engagements," explains Jay Goldberg of The SportsMakers Agency, L.L.C. "Normally, a company will approach the sports agent seeking an athlete. Occasionally, if the agent is affiliated with a particular athlete, it can work the other way with the agent promoting the athlete to a prospective sponsor. The agent is paid between 10-30% of the contract amount for his services."

### ■ ■ ■ A Sports Agent Unites Mark Leone and Loro Piana

Mark Leone had enjoyed five years of corporate sponsorship prior to being approached by Karen Powell, Executive Vice President of The Pinewood Corporation, on behalf of Ing. Loro Piana & C.

The Pinewood Corporation is a sports agency with offices in New York and Toronto. They represent a number of individual athletes in the equestrian, race car driving, and triathlon disciplines and assist these individuals in securing sponsorships and seeking out publicity opportunities.

Pinewood is retained by corporations to assist in strategic sports marketing planning, sponsorship negotiation and securement, publicity securement, client entertainment, and hospitality planning. The firm's principles have developed strategic marketing programs for multinational corporations including the Seagrams Company, Ing. Loro Piana & C., Audi, Magna International, and NCR.

### ■ ■ ■ Ing. Loro Piana & C.

Ing. Loro Piana & C. (henceforth, Loro Piana) is the world's leading manufacturer of quality cashmeres, worsteds, yarns, and accessories. The company buys, spins, and weaves vicuna from Peru, cashmere from China and Mongolia, and wool from Tasmania and Australia – all from its state-of-the-art facilities in the United States, China, and Italy. One of its many finished goods is the *horsey jacket*, which was designed with the assistance of, and for use by, the Italian Equestrian Team in the 1992 Barcelona Summer Olympics.

Loro Piana sponsors riders in Europe – including Italian Equestrian Team riders Filippo Moyersoen and Roberto Arioldi, and the father and son team Nelson and Rodrigo Pessoa. Loro Piana sponsors equestrian events because the demographics of the equestrian audience are ideal: exclusive, upscale, high-income. Unlike traditional marketing where there is dilution of the communications medium, equestrian sports enable Loro Piana to speak directly to their target market.

### ■ ■ ■ Loro Piana's Show Jumping Sponsorship Objectives

Loro Piana has three objectives in sponsoring Mark Leone and his stable of horses:

1. to receive media exposure throughout the show season through their association with Mark's horses and through his interaction with the media;

2. to generate interest and awareness in the Loro Piana brand and its products within the equestrian community; and

3. to be associated with an exclusive high-end sport.

## ■ ■ ■ Loro Piana's Reasons for Selecting Mark Leone

Loro Piana was seeking a top horse and rider combination in the United States to represent them. Although the sponsorship was discussed with several USET riders, Loro Piana and The Pinewood Corporation felt that Mark Leone had the most to offer. In addition to his talent and experience competing jumpers, he also offered depth and breadth of horses. Mark could deliver the benefits of four top horses. "In addition, he is athletic, attractive, and a very talented commentator," says Karen. "He is articulate and someone whom the media look to for comment because he is so well-spoken. Mark is the All-American success story who understands the needs of his sponsor and is always willing to go the extra mile. For instance, last winter he brought a horse into Manhattan for a media shoot in front of the Loro Piana shop on East 61st Street."

Karen goes on to say, "Although talent and athletic skill are the number one priority, attractive personality traits such as honesty, humor, interpersonal skills, communications skills, and commitment to the sponsorship are evaluated."

Name recognition is an important factor in finding corporate sponsorship; however, Karen explains that "ability, international accomplishments and winnings, credibility, integrity, depth and breadth of horses are also important factors." She continues, "the age of a rider is secondary. The most important factor is whether they have established a name for themselves as a winner and have a history of proven results; young or old, age is irrelevant."

## ■ ■ ■ The Pinewood Corporation

The Pinewood Corporation became involved with equestrian sponsorships when Karen Powell came on board in 1990. Karen has an Honors Degree in Business Administration from the University of Western Ontario and is fluent in both French and English. She has worked in each of the firm's three functional areas; marketing and communications, entertainment and event marketing, and representation and agentry.

Karen's riding and educational background are strong assets. She rode on the "A" rated show jumping circuit for ten years, and won the overall junior championship against older and more experienced riders when she was only 12 years old. Her numerous awards include two silver medals at the North American Continental Young Riders' Championships. Karen's equine involvement also extended to training grand prix show jumpers for international competition under the tutelage of Hugh Graham. One of her horses, Wellington, whom she bought as a seven-year-old to be her junior jumper, developed to the Grand Prix level and secured the team gold at the Pan American Games in 1987.

If the idea of using a sports agent appeals to you, it is important that you find out as much as possible about the agency and its representatives before signing any contracts. It will save you a lot of time in the long run, and you are assured at the outset that you are dealing with people who speak the same language – horses!

# Insurance

Approximately half of the sponsors and sponsorees interviewed insure their horses. They all carry mortality insurance while some carry major medical, surgical, and loss of use as well.

Whatever your own feelings are regarding insuring a horse, you should bring insurance issues to the attention of your sponsor – especially if your sponsor is not a knowledgeable horse person.

Although most policies are written on an annual basis, it is possible to get short term policies. Rates are based on the animal's age, sex, breed, and use and are stated as a percentage of the insured value.

Insurance options include:

- full mortality: accident, illness, disease
- specified perils: fire, lightning, smoke
- specified and optional perils
- special accident
- theft
- agreed value/guaranteed renewal for breeding stock

- first season infertility
- prospective foal
- barrenness/prospective foal/stallion availability

Read policies carefully and be aware that there are time limits within which you must report an accident, euthanasia, surgery, etc. Otherwise, the policy will be void.

Policies and rates vary from agency to agency. You will have to do some research in order to find the best coverage at the best rates.

# Rules and Restrictions for Sponsored Riders Competing Internationally

For sponsored riders planning to compete internationally or in the Olympics, it is imperative that you be aware of rules governing sponsorships and how sponsorships can affect your status as a competitor.

> *Sponsorship agreements that do not adhere to IOC (International Olympic Committee) and FEI (Federation Equestre Internationale) rules could change your status as an amateur to that of a professional, thereby preventing you from competing in certain competitions, including but not limited to the Olympics.*

The AHSA (American Horse Shows Association) is our National Federation (NF) and "is responsible to the FEI for the compliance of U.S. competitors with FEI rules; however, the FEI has ultimate responsibility for the interpretation of its rules, and it is the FEI rules, not the AHSA guidelines, that will govern the outcome of any dispute or controversy."

The AHSA has an excellent pamphlet entitled *Guidelines on Eligibility & Sponsorship for Competitors Entering International Events – Advice for Riders & Sponsors.* Topics that the AHSA pamphlet covers include:

- Explanation of the difference between a professional and an amateur

- Competitions that professionals may not compete in

- Reclassification of a rider's status

- Advertising restrictions

- Rules on logos (size and placement)

- Changing a horse's name (e.g., adding a prefix to the name to indicate the sponsoring company)

- Handling of sponsorship funds by the AHSA including administrative fees

- Information on when you don't need an AHSA agreement

- Responsibility of the competitor to know and abide by the AHSA's rules regarding sponsorships

- Limitations of the AHSA's responsibilities

You may call or write the AHSA to request a copy of the abovementioned pamphlet. Their address and phone number are:

International Department
American Horse Shows Association, Inc.
220 East 42nd Street - Suite 409
New York, NY 10017-5876
tel. 212-972-2472  fax 212-983-7286

The AHSA advises all people who are contemplating sponsorships to consult their tax advisors before entering into any agreement. And, because rules can and do change, it is the responsibility of the sponsoree to stay current on sponsorship rules and regulations.

## ■ ■ ■ Amateurs and Professionals

Refer to the *AHSA Rule Book*, Article 808 Amateur Status and Article 810 Professional Status for a thorough definition of what constitutes an amateur and a professional. These rules are only applicable to riders competing nationally.

## ■ ■ ■ The Federation Equestre Internationale (FEI)

The FEI has extensive rules and regulations governing sponsored riders. Everything from licensing to sponsorship agreements to publicity and more. You should contact them directly for the most up-to-date rules and regulations.

# Scholarships

# Scholarships

There are at least four types of scholarship available to equestrians:

1. riding scholarships through riding clubs
2. riding scholarships through breed organizations
3. educational scholarships through breed organizations
4. scholarships as prizes

Riding scholarships through riding clubs and riding scholarships through breed organizations are available to equestrians to enhance their riding educations. Educational scholarships through breed organizations are available to riders needing financial aid to pursue advanced academic or vocational training. Only active members are eligible for these scholarships.

The following sections describe these scholarships as well as specific organizations offering them.

# Riding Club Scholarship Funds

Riding clubs nationwide are realizing that knowledge gained by any one of their members is beneficial to the club as a whole, and many clubs are embracing the idea of making scholarship funds available to their members. Riding clubs across the country, from small grassroots organizations to much larger national organizations, have scholarship money available to their members.

Some clubs publicize their scholarship activities better than others. If you are not sure whether your club has a scholarship fund, call or write one of your board members. If no fund exists, make a motion for the club to form one. Scholarship funds are easy to form and to administer and can be gratifying for all involved.

## ■ ■ ■ Forming a Scholarship Fund

Forming a fund requires getting your board and members to agree on creating a scholarship fund. Then they need to organize and decide how to implement and administer the fund. A scholarship committee should be formed, and they will need to determine:

- how to raise money for the scholarship fund
- eligibility requirements
- deadlines for applications
- when and how to distribute money
- selection criteria
- how much money to give to recipients based on the recipients' requests and available funds

Requirements for eligibility vary from club to club, with active membership being the single requirement shared by all. Several organizations require scholarship recipients to have been active, dues paying members for a minimum of one year, while others require their members to volunteer at the club's shows, clinics, demonstrations, or wherever they may be helpful.

## ■ ■ ■ Administering a Scholarship Fund

It is usual for clubs to form a Scholarship Committee to administer the club's scholarship fund. In many cases, the committees change from year to year. Committee members typically review scholarship requests individually and then meet as a group to decide who to give money to and in what amounts.

Members who do not receive money are encouraged to reapply the following year. Some clubs do not award money to the same person more than once.

## ■ ■ ■ Source of Funds

Breed organizations and riding clubs have various means for raising money for their scholarship funds:

- Proceeds from horse shows
- Interest from Certificates of Deposit
- Donations from members
- Proceeds from tack sales or any other type of club-sponsored sales
- Fundraising events such as demonstrations

## ■ ■ ■ Reserve Fund

A number of clubs have reserve funds to handle special requests. For example, if a club member is eligible to compete in a year-end championship, or to receive special training, then the club may choose to assist the rider financially.

# Educational Riding Scholarships

Several organizations offer scholarships to enable their members to enhance their equestrian educations.

## ■ ■ ■ American Morgan Horse Institute

The American Morgan Horse Institute, Inc. (AMHI) encourages excellence in youth by providing scholarships to outstanding young men and women. The American Morgan Horse Institute, through the American Morgan Horse Association (AMHA), offers its members two scholarship funds: The Van Schaik Scholarship described below and the Dressage Scholarship, which is described in the section entitled *Scholarships as Awards*.

### The Van Schaik Scholarship
The Van Schaik Scholarship is available to members riding Morgans at the lower levels, but with aspirations of moving up through the dressage levels. This fund distributes $1,000 per year to AMHA members competing in dressage. More detailed information on the AMHA scholarship programs may be obtained by contacting Lisa Peterson at

the American Morgan Horse Association, P.O. Box 960, Shelburne, VT 05482-0960; tel. 802-985-4944.

# ■ ■ ■ American Trakehner Association

### The Terry Koenig Memorial Fund

The Terry Koenig Memorial Fund was established in 1992 in memory of FEI dressage trainer/rider/competitor, Terry Koenig.

This scholarship is available to junior/young riders who are members of the American Trakehner Association and are competing either a Trakehner or part-Trakehner. The rider may be competing in any discipline and is eligible for the award more than once. Each year one rider is selected by the Awards Committee with the approval of the Executive Committee of the ATA to receive this scholarship.

For more information on this scholarship and how to apply, contact Charee Adams, American Trakehner Association, 1520 W. Church Street, Newark, OH 44320; Tel. No. 614-344-1111; Fax 614-344-3225

# ■ ■ ■ The Carl-Heinrich Asmis Scholarship Fund

The purpose of the Carl-Heinrich Asmis Scholarship Fund is to help dedicated riders who are willing, after completion of the scholarship, to further the interest of dressage and the Carl-Heinrich Asmis Scholarship Fund. The Scholarship must be spent in the study of dressage abroad and is available to anyone riding Fourth level or above. A rider who wants to apply for the Scholarship must belong to a sponsoring organization who can supply him/her with the application form.

Since its inception in 1974, the Carl-Heinrich Asmis Scholarship Fund has helped such well-known riders as Elizabeth Lewis, Lendon Gray, Carol Lavell, and Michelle Gibson advance their training.

More detailed information is available by contacting C-H Asmis Dressage Scholarship Fund, Never Die Farm, 6150 Emerald Lane, Sykesville, MD 21784

# ■ ■ ■ The Dressage Foundation, Inc.

The Dressage Foundation, Inc. is a significant source of funds for aspiring dressage riders. Their mission statement, which follows, says it best:

"The Dressage Foundation Inc. is dedicated to the advancement and support of classical dressage. It was established in the belief that dressage provides the fundamental discipline and training needed to achieve a high standard in all forms of equestrian activities, regardless of breed or discipline.

"The Foundation's mission is to provide for the long term support of dressage in the United States, mainly through the programs and activities of the United States Dressage Federation. It seeks to provide access to educational opportunities for equestrians without regard to race, sex, religion or national origin, in order for them to achieve maximum competency in dressage.

"The Dressage Foundation works to establish long term, financially stable ways for individuals, organizations, and private businesses to support dressage and is recognized by the U.S. Treasury as a 501(c)3 non-profit educational organization."

As can be seen from The Foundation's mission statement, this is an organization dedicated to the long-term goals of dressage education in the United States. To meet these goals, The Foundation offers a number of individual and corporate funds.

## Individual Funds

**Violet M. Hopkins Dressage Fund** – $50,000 has been dedicated to this fund to help promote good, sound instructional programs through USDF Group Member Organizations (GMO). In 1995, $2,650 was distributed among four recipients enrolled in various educational dressage programs. Applications are available only to GMOs and can be obtained from The Dressage Foundation.

**John P. Kimball Education Fund** – this fund was started in 1994. Its goal is to promote dressage in the southeastern United States.

**Ivan Bezugloff Literary Fund** – for authors who write articles on the technical aspects of dressage.

**ReSolutions Farm Fund** – Martha and Jon Driscoll started this fund to help young and amateur riders in the northwest area.

**Region 6 Young Riders Fund** – this fund is used as a depository for donations received from Region 6.

**Major Andres Lindgren Scholarship** – this $6,000 annual scholarship is for recipients to use to improve their dressage riding, teaching, and training skills. Study must take place abroad.

## Corporate Funds

Members Long Distance Advantage, Trotting Park Workshop, MBNA America, Miller Harness Company, Interland Group, American Bankers Insurance Company have provided support to The Dressage Foundation by donating raffles, royalties, or a percentage of their charges.

### The Benefactors Club

The Benefactors Club is a means by which individuals and corporations can financially support The Dressage Foundation. It was started in 1990 and serves as the base of support for Foundation activities. At the end of 1995, there were 52 Benefactors who donated or pledged $1,000.

For more detailed information on The Dressage Foundation and their scholarships, contact them at:

> The Dressage Foundation
> 130 North Tenth Street
> Lincoln, NE 68508
> Tel. 402-434-8586  Fax 402-434-8545

# Educational Scholarships
# Through Breed Organizations

Several breed organizations offer educational scholarships to their members. The following list of organizations that have educational scholarship programs is not exhaustive. If you are a member of a breed organization not listed here, contact your club directly for information on scholarships.

- American Morgan Horse Institute
- American Paint Horse Association
- American Quarter Horse Youth Association
- American Saddlebred Horse Association
- Appaloosa Youth Foundation
- International Arabian Horse Foundation
- International Buckskin Horse Association
- Palomino Horse Breeders Association
- Pony of the Americas Club, Inc.

- Welsh Pony & Cob Foundation

The following overviews describe the scholarship programs offered by these breed organizations. Along with the completed application form, most of these organizations require letters of recommendation, a photograph of the applicant, proof of financial need, school transcripts, and information regarding the applicant's extracurricular activities. Once the organization's scholarship committee has decided to whom they will award scholarship money, they contact the recipient directly and send the funds to the educational institution that the recipient specifies. For the most up-to-date information and application forms, please contact the organization directly.

## ■ ■ ■ American Morgan Horse Institute, Inc.

Dane Bettes
AMHI Scholarships
7112 County Road 802
Burleson, TX 76028

| | |
|---|---|
| Number of recipients | Five per year |
| Amount distributed | $3,000 each |
| Application deadline | March 1 of the year in which the recipient would like to receive a scholarship |
| Types of scholarships | Academic and Vocational |

Eligibility

The program is open to anyone who is/will be a high school graduate/ GED. Previous winners of an AMHI Scholarship are ineligible to participate a second time. Previous applicants who did not win a scholarship may re-apply. Selection is based on the ability and aptitude for serious study, community service, leadership, financial need, and achievement with horses. The following criteria are taken into consideration when awarding these scholarships:

- the applicant has completed or is involved in the American Morgan Horse Association (AMHA) Horsemastership Program, or
- the applicant is involved in a 4H/FFA program, or

- the applicant has won an AHSA and/or AMHA Medal for equitation, or

- the applicant has placed in the top two in the junior division or the top four in the adult division of an open competition program.

## ■ ■ ■ American Paint Horse Association

Ed Roberts, Executive Secretary
P.O. Box 961023
Fort Worth, TX 76161-0023
(817) 439-3400  Fax (817) 439-3484

| | |
|---|---|
| Number of recipients | 15 for the 1995-1996 school year |
| Amount distributed | Not more than $1,000 per person per year |
| Application deadline | April 1 of the year in which applicant wishes to receive the grant |
| Types of scholarships | Academic and Vocational. Academic $1,000 yearly. Must have a "B" average or its equivalent (3.0). May be renewable through an applicant's fifth year of schooling if "B" grade point average is maintained. Vocational $1,000 yearly. Must have a "B" grade or its equivalent (3.0). This scholarship is for two years if "B" grade point average is maintained. Applicant can re-apply at the end of second year. |
| Scholarship founded | 1981 |
| Organization | IRS 501(c)3 |
| Special note | children of the YDF Board or the Executive Committee Board are not eligible for these scholarships. |

Eligibility

The applicant must be a current APHA member who has been active in the Paint industry for at least one year prior to time of application; be a high school graduate or equivalent; show evidence of financial need; and indicate whether they are applying for the Academic or Vocational Scholarship.

## ■ ■ ■ American Quarter Horse Foundation

Heath Miller, Director of Youth Activities & AQHYA
1600 Quarter Horse Drive
Amarillo, TX 79104
806-376-4811

As of early 1996, the AQHA scholarship program had served 420 students and distributed nearly $500,000 in scholarships.

| | |
|---|---|
| Number of recipients | 34 for the 1995-1996 school year |
| Amount distributed | Not more than $1,000 per person per year |
| Application deadline | May 15 of the year in which the applicant wishes to receive a scholarship |
| Scholarship founded | 1976 |
| Organization | IRS 501(c)3 |
| Special note | Individuals are eligible for a maximum of four years of funding. They must maintain a 2.5 GPA and be enrolled as a full-time student during the semester(s) for which the scholarship is funded. |

Eligibility
Applicant must be a member in good standing of the AQHYA (AJQHA) during the last two years; be 21 years of age or under as of January 1 of the year in which he/she is applying for scholarship funding; and show evidence of financial need.

## ■ ■ ■ American Saddlebred Horse Association Foundation Scholarship

Amy L. Burns, ASHA Youth Coordinator
4093 Iron Works Pike
Lexington, KY 40511
606-259-2742  Fax 606-259-1628

Scholarships are awarded one time only to any individual. Scholarship applications may be resubmitted annually.

| | |
|---|---|
| Number of recipients | Six per year |
| Amount distributed | Approximately $6,000 annually |
| Application deadline | April 30 of the year the applicant wishes to receive the scholarship |
| Scholarship founded | 1991 |
| Organization | IRS 501(c)3 |
| Special Note | New scholarship as of 1996 – Salem-Teikyo University in Salem, WV is offering two $2,000 renewable scholarships to applicants who attend STU and who maintain a 3.0 grade point average. |

Eligibility

Applicant must be an ASHA member; be 21 years old or younger; be at grade 11 or higher; and show evidence of financial need.

# ■ ■ ■ Appaloosa Youth Foundation Scholarship Committee

Keri Minden, ApHC Youth Coordinator
P.O. Box 8403, 5070 Hwy 8 West
Moscow, ID 83843
208-882-5578  Fax 208-882-8150

| | |
|---|---|
| Number of recipients | 11-12 per year |
| Amount distributed | Approximately $12,000 annually |
| Application deadline | June 10 of the year in which the applicant wishes to receive a scholarship |
| Types of scholarships | Appaloosa Youth Foundation (AYF) Educational Scholarship and Sagebrush Circuit Educational Scholarship. |
| The AYF Scholarship | is typically for someone just entering college, but this is not a requirement. |

| The Sagebrush Circuit | is for students studying in an equine-related field who are in their junior or senior year in their undergraduate program, or in graduate school. (One scholarship is awarded annually in the amount of $2,000.) |
|---|---|
| Scholarship founded | 1971 |
| Organization | IRS 501(c)3 |
| Special note | Members of the immediate family of an employee, representative, or National Director of the ApHC are not eligible for either of these scholarships. |

Eligibility

Applicant must be a member of the Appaloosa Horse Club or the Appaloosa Youth Association, and the application must be endorsed by an ApHC affiliated regional club or racing association.

## ■ ■ ■ International Arabian Horse Foundation

Jim Cada, President
10805 E. Bethany Drive
Aurora, CO 80014
303-696-4500   Fax 303-696-4599

The IAHA has given various scholarship awards as prizes through the International Arabian Horse Association since its incorporation in 1950 and has had various scholarship funds and educational grants available to applicants since IAHF's incorporation in 1975.

| Number of recipients | Varies each year. In 1995, 47 individuals received scholarships by competing or judging at International Arabian Horse Association sponsored shows. |
|---|---|
| Amount distributed | $47,000 in 1995 |
| Application deadline | May 1 of the year in which the applicant wishes to receive the scholarship |
| Scholarship founded | 1950 |

| Organization | IRS 501(c)3 |
| --- | --- |
| Special note | The International Arabian Horse Foundation funds six active scholarships, and the scholarships can be applied for by individuals of any age. |

Eligibility

Members of IAHA or owners of Arabian and half-Arabian horses. Scholarships are awarded on the basis of academic ability, leadership, financial need, and involvement in equine activities.

## ■ ■ ■ International Buckskin Horse Association, Inc.

Richard E. Kurzeja
P.O. Box 268
Shelby, IN 46377-0268
219-552-1013

| Number of recipients | 6 to 10 per year |
| --- | --- |
| Amount distributed | between $1,000 and $1,500 per award |
| Scholarship founded | 1987 |
| Organization | IRS 501(c)3 |

Eligibility

Applicant must have been an active youth member for the two years previous to applying and also in the current year of applying. He/she must have a "B" average to qualify and must maintain the "B" average to renew for continued support.

## ■ ■ ■ Palomino Horse Breeders of America Youth Scholarship & Educational Fund

K. Dwayne Beck, President
15253 E. Skelly Drive
Tulsa, OK 74116-2637
(918) 438-1234

| | |
|---|---|
| Scholarship founded | 1995 |
| Organization | IRS 501(c)3 |

## ■ ■ ■ Pony of the Americas Club Scholarship Endowment Fund, Inc.

Jean Kelley, Executive Secretary Pro Tem
5240 Elmwood Avenue
Indianapolis, IN 46203
(317) 788-0107

The Pony of the Americas Scholarship Endowment Fund is a separate non-profit corporation from the Pony of the Americas Club, Inc.

| | |
|---|---|
| Number of recipients | Two to four per year |
| Amount distributed | Dependent on how much money is available in any given year |
| Application deadline | Postmarked no later than June 1 and received no later than June 10 to be considered for a scholarship that year |
| Scholarship founded | Circa 1975 |
| Organization | IRS 501(c)3 |

Eligibility
   Applicant must be a member of a POA family who is either a graduating senior, or attending an institute of higher learning such as a trade school, junior college, university, etc.

## ■ ■ ■ Welsh Pony & Cob Society of America

Ms. Lisa L. Landis
P.O. Box 2977
Winchester, VA 22601-2977
540-667-6195

| | |
|---|---|
| Number of recipients | Usually two per year |
| Amount distributed | $500 per recipient |

| | |
|---|---|
| Application deadline | September 15 of the year in which the recipient would like to receive a scholarship |
| Scholarship founded | 1987 |
| Organization | IRS 501(c)3 |

Eligibility

Applicant must be a citizen of the United States; must graduate high school during year of award, or be in college or professional school; must demonstrate satisfactory academic performance; and must submit information on past involvement in equine-related activities. Selection is based on the candidate's past performance, both as a student and as an equestrian. Grades to be submitted include Junior and Senior years in high school, and if candidate is currently a college student, include grades up to present time. Candidates should also list non equine-related activities associated both with school and outside of school.

## ■ ■ ■ What IRS 501(c)3 Means

501(c)3 is a status assigned by the Internal Revenue Service indicating that an organization is not-for-profit. Donations made to 501(c)3 organizations are tax deductible.

# Scholarships as Awards

## ■■■ American Hackney Horse Society

Kathy Schultz
4059 Iron Works Pike, Building A
Lexington, KY 40511
606-255-8694  Fax 606-255-0177

The American Hackney Horse Society Foundation offers significant cash prizes at the Youth Medallion Championship competition, which is held in November of each year. The prize money is to be used for tuition at an accredited college of the recipient's choice. Four prizes of $500 each are awarded to the winners of the Roadster Pony, Pleasure Driving Pony, Roadster Pony Under Saddle, and Hackney/Harness Combination Classes.

To be eligible, competitors must not have reached their 18th birthday as of December 1 of the current competition year and must be competing a registered Hackney. This prize money may be won by the same person more than once.

## ■ ■ ■ American Morgan Horse Institute

### The Dressage Scholarship

The Dressage Scholarship is an award of $2,500 and can be earned only once by any rider. To qualify for this award, a rider must obtain five Grand Prix dressage scores with a median of 60% or higher from at least four different USDF recognized competitions from four different judges. All scores do not have to be attained in one year. Money awarded from this scholarship must be used for educational purposes.

More detailed information on the AMHA scholarship programs may be obtained by contacting Lisa Peterson at the American Morgan Horse Association, P.O. Box 960, Shelburne, VT 05482-0960; tel. 802-985-4944.

## ■ ■ ■ National Reining Horse Association

448 Main Street, #204
Coshocton, OH 43812-1200
614-623-0055

### Team Competition Scholarship Award

The National Reining Horse Association awards scholarships to the first three placings in a three member team tournament that is held during the NRHA Derby and Superstakes every June in Oklahoma City, OK. Members may ride any breed horse, and each member of the winning team receives a scholarship toward the school of his/her choice. Teams consist of three riders, one of whom must be in the 13 and under age group. The top three teams are awarded prize money as follows:

| | |
|---|---|
| 1st place | $3,000 (divided equally among the three team members) |
| 2nd place | $1,500 (divided equally among the three team members) |
| 3rd place | $750 (divided equally among the three team members) |

Recipients are responsible for apprising their colleges of the money won, which is then forwarded to the college from the NRHA.

### John McQuay Memorial Scholarship

This is a scholarship awarded to the winner of the Youth 13 and Under class at the NRHA Derby and Superstakes.

### Youth Incentive Award

The Paul Horn Youth Memorial was started by friends and family of Paul Horn, the 1973 NHRA Futurity Champion riding King J Bar. This $500 cash prize is awarded to the highest scoring youth in the two combined classes: the 13 year old and under age group, and the 14-18 year old age group.

## ■ ■ ■ Maria Caleel Memorial Fund

United States Equestrian Team, Inc.
Route 512
Gladstone, NJ 07934
908-234-1251

The Maria Caleel Memorial Fund was created by friends, family, and associates of Maria Caleel and is administered by the United States Equestrian Team.

Maria was active in show jumping competitions for a number of years and later developed an interest in dressage. This is a cash award given to the winner of the Intermediare I Dressage Championship. The money is to be used for training with the trainer of the winner's choice approved by the USET.

## ■ ■ ■ National High School Rodeo Association

DeeDee Huff
11178 N. Huron, Suite #7
Denver, CO 80234
303-452-0820 fax 303-452-0912

The National High School Rodeo Association (NHSRA) is an international, non-profit organization dedicated to the development of sportsmanship, horsemanship, and character in the youth of our countries. It has nearly 13,000 members from 38 U.S. states and four Canadian provinces. In 1947, Claude Mullins founded the NHSRA on two principles: to encourage our youth to stay in school and to promote the highest type of conduct and sportsmanship.

The NHSRA has numerous sponsors including DeWALT, Dodge Truck Rodeo, Featherlite Trailers, HealthSouth, Laredo Boots, B-C Rodeo Awards, Gist, Inc., Lancaster's Rock n'Roll Rodeo Gear, Looking for 8 Saddle and Tack,

North American Corriente Assn., Elbauer Brothers, Courts Saddlery, CLG PRO Rodeo Products, Resistol Hats, Wrangler, the Professional Rodeo Cowboys Association, the American Quarter Horse Assocation, the National Cutting Horse Association, and Woody's Feeds.

Scholarship prize money is awarded at the annual National High School Finals Rodeo (NHSFR). Boys All-Around Champion, Girls All-Around Champion, Girl & Boy Rookies of the Year, and Timed Events, are just a sampling of the events that award scholarship prize money.

In addition to scholarships in the form of prize money, NHSRA has an educational scholarship program. NHSFR senior qualifiers can apply for scholarships based on financial need and academic excellence. In 1995, NSHRA awarded $106,000 in scholarships.

## ■ ■ ■ USDF/Purina Mills, Inc. Junior/Young Rider Scholarship Program

United States Dressage Federation, Inc.
P.O. Box 6669
Lincoln, NE 68506-0669
402-434-8550

Purina Mills, Inc., through the United States Dressage Federation, is providing educational assistance to young dressage riders nationwide. The program was founded in 1994, and in 1995, nine scholarships totalling $3,450 were awarded to first place winners of USDF Junior/Young Rider Awards.

Recipients of these cash prizes may use the money for any aspect of their dressage education including clinics, lessons with a local trainer, or a college dressage program.

Cash awards in 1995 were awarded to division champions as follows:

- Training - Second level                $250 each

- Third - Fourth level                    $350 each

- Prix St. Georges - Grand Prix           $500 each

To be eligible for these awards, riders must be USDF members under 21 years of age and adhere to the USDF's rules regarding the Horse of the Year Awards program. Contact the USDF at the address above for more detailed information on this program.

# Final Note

When researching this book, it was my intention to get a good cross-section of equestrians from as many different disciplines as possible. Although most of the sponsored riders had similar goals, there was a lot of variation in how they achieved their goals. This book is not, nor is intended to be, the last word in finding sponsorship. Instead, it is meant to highlight the availability of sponsorship opportunities and to explain some of the methods that have been employed with success.

Whenever the opportunity presents itself, I strongly urge you to talk with any and every sponsored rider you meet in your travels. Undoubtedly, you will discover even more ways to raise money for your equestrian endeavors by speaking with sponsored riders, and they may describe methods that are better suited to your personality type.

There is no doubt that plenty of money is available from both the private and the corporate sectors. It is your task to select the fundraising method that best suits you and then establish persuasive enough reasons so that you can obtain access to these funds.

# Index

## A

AHSA 145
American Horse Shows Association.
  *See* AHSA
American Morgan Horse Institute, Inc.
  162, 172
American Paint Horse Association 163
American Quarter Horse Foundation
  164
American Saddlebred Horse Associa-
  tion Foundation Society 164
American Trakehner Association 158
Appaloosa Youth Foundation Scholar-
  ship Committee 165

## B

Beval, Ltd. 117–120
Blacklow, Haley 127
Budget 30

## C

Centennial Farm 45
Centennial Farms 56
Corporate sponsors 16, 107, 127
Coward, Marindi 49–53
Craven, John 116
Crown Royal 60

## D

De Rosa, Diana 111
Demographics 111, 130, 131
Dodge Truck Rodeo 129-131
Dressage Foundation, Inc. 158
Dymar Agency 128

## E

East Hill Farm 73

## F

FEI 145, 147

## G

Gibson, Michelle 39–44
Goldberg, Jay 139
Goodman, Dr. & Mrs. David 86
Goodman, Pat 86, 89
Grigg, Natasha 121–126

## H

Hamilton, John 128
Hampton Classic Horse Show 111–114
Hitchcock, Anthony 111
Hogan-Poulsen, Ruth 73–78

## I

Insurance 143
International Arabian Horse Founda-
  tion 166
International Buckskin Horse Associa-
  tion, Inc. 167
IRS 501(c)3 169

## J

John Madden Sales, Inc. 80

## K

Kanavy, Valerie 67–72
Kulski, Lisa 91–95

## L

Leone, Mark 59, 140–142
Lindgren, Jean 111
Little, Donald V. Jr. 55–58

Loro Piana 62, 140–142
Lowry, Jack 129
Lyons, John 50

## M

Maria Caleel Memorial Fund 173
Miller Harness Company 115

## N

National High School Rodeo Association 173
National Reining Horse Association 172
New England Equestrian Center 91
Non-profit organizations 169

## P

Palomino Horse Breeders of America Youth Scholarship 167
Patton, Beezie 79–83, 118
Pinewood Corporation 62, 141–142
Pony of the Americas Club Scholarship Endowment Fund 168
Poulin, Larry 122–126
Powell, Karen 62
PRCA 129, 133–136
Private sponsors 16, 108
Professional Rodeo Cowboy Association. *See* PRCA
Proposal 27
  budget 30
  competition record 31
  creating a 27
  plan 29
  resume 29
  testimonials 31
  videos and photographs 31

## R

Rader, Richard 85–89

Ri-Arm Farm 59
Rules and restrictions 145–146
  amateurs and professionals 147

## S

Sample Budget 30
Scholarships 157, 161
  academic 161, 163
    American Morgan Horse Institute, Inc. 162
    American Paint Horse Association 163
    American Quarter Horse Foundation 164
    American Saddlebred Horse Association Foundation 164
    Appaloosa Youth Foundation 165
    International Arabian Horse Foundation 166
    International Buckskin Horse Association 167
    Palomino Horse Breeders of America 167
    Pony of the Americas 168
    Welsh Pony & Cob Society of America 168
  As awards 171
    American Hackney Horse Society 171
    Dressage Scholarship 172
    Maria Caleel Memorial Fund 173
    National High School Rodeo Association 173
    National Reining Horse Association 172
    USDF/Purina Mills, Inc. Junior/Young Rider 174
  Educational riding 157
    American Morgan Horse Institute 157

American Trakehner Association 158

Carl-Heinrich Asmis 158

Major Andres Lindgren 159

Region 6 Young Riders Fund 159

ReSolutions Farm Fund 159

Terry Koenig Memorial 158

The Dressage Foundation, Inc. 158

Van Schaik 157

Violet M. Hopkins Dressage Fund 159

  Ivan Bezugloff Literary Fund 159

  John P. Kimball 159

  Riding club 153

Shrake, Lee Ann 98

Shrake, Richard 97–104

Sports agents 139–142

Sportsmaker's Agency 139

Stadium Jumping, Inc. 120

Stateline Tack 127

Stephens, Debbie Shaffner 45–48

## U

USDF/Purina Mills, Inc. Junior/Young Rider Scholarship 174

## W

Walter, Mark 117

Welsh Pony & Cob Society of America 168

Winning Way Ltd. 98

Wrangler World of Rodeo 134